Walking with GOD Is a Divine Journey

Spiritual development involves growing through life's experiences

Lisa Olivares Young

iUniverse, Inc.
Bloomington

Walking with God Is a Divine Journey
Spiritual Development through Life's Experiences

iUniverse books may be ordered through booksellers or by contacting:

iUniverse
1663 Liberty Drive
Bloomington, IN 47403
www.iuniverse.com
1-800-Authors (1-800-288-4677)

Because of the dynamic nature of the Internet, any web addresses or links contained in this book may have changed since publication and may no longer be valid. The views expressed in this work are solely those of the author and do not necessarily reflect the views of the publisher, and the publisher hereby disclaims any responsibility for them.

Any people depicted in stock imagery provided by Thinkstock are models, and such images are being used for illustrative purposes only.

Certain stock imagery © Thinkstock.

ISBN: 978-1-4759-0593-9 (sc)
ISBN: 978-1-4759-0591-5 (e)
ISBN: 978-1-4759-0592-2 (dj)

Library of Congress Control Number: 2012906099

Printed in the United States of America

iUniverse rev. date: 4/19/2012

Dedication

This book is dedicated to my children Danielle and Tyrone, who have inspired me to embrace life and learning with everything in me that I may be a better mother, teacher and role model for them!

Preface

This book is about spiritual growth and a true testimony to how everything in your life happens for a reason. Life's experiences and circumstances, which we most times view as overwhelming obstacles are designed to teach us, mold us, and develop us toward the will of God. God will often use your life experiences to get your attention and to awaken your thoughts and spirit to acknowledge him for your good; He will also use your experiences to build you in character for the uplifting of his kingdom, that you may be a living example for the rest of the world.

The Great Commission

"Then the eleven disciples went to Galilee, to the mountain where Jesus had told them to go. When they saw him, they worshiped him; but some doubted. Then Jesus came to them and said, "All authority in heaven and on earth has been given to me. Therefore go and make disciples of all nations, baptizing them in the name of the Father and of the Son and of the Holy Spirit, and teaching them to obey everything I have commanded you. And surely I am with you always, to the very end of the age." (Matthew 28:16-20)

Contents

Introduction   xi

Chapter I: Life's journey   1

    Life is a wakeup call   3
    Life as a teacher   6
    The Past does not dictate your future   10

Chapter II: Knowledge and Growth   15

    How to Learn from your past   17
    Mistakes create an opportunity for a victorious comeback   20
    Learning is a never ending journey   23
    Life-long learning enhances your vision   26
    The Ability to Learn and Unlearn   28

Chapter III: Life is about Change   33

    Move When the World Moves Around You!   35
    Overcoming Life's Challenges   40
    Waiting by Faith   43

Chapter IV: Life Convoy   49

    People and Choices   51

The road less traveled!   55

Transition: Stages of Spiritual development   61

Discovering your purpose   67

Renewing Your Mind!   69

Chapter V: Faith restores vision   71

Purpose to move forward   73

Your hearts desire   78

Embrace your dreams by creating goals to get you there   81

Sometimes life's set-backs are merely a Set-up!   84

Building a Better Relationship with God   88

Learning to Receive God's Correction   93

Profound Peace   96

References   103

Index   107

Introduction

Life in its many forms has one constant that it is forever changing. Webster's defines change as "transition from one state of being to another" (186). As we enter life at birth we begin growth stages that come in intervals and propel us into a disparity of developmental phases, from infancy well into adulthood. It is through these various stages of growth that we develop a foundation for who we will become. Some of these qualities and characteristics are innate, simply a part of our DNA however, other faculties are ones we learn along the way. Our features change as do our personalities and attitudes towards life as we know it, but as we grow and learn to face these inevitable changes head on, we then learn to overcome and adjust with time.

In our life's journey we will undoubtedly be faced with choices and decision that will mold us into who we are and how we will live. Sometimes God places us in situations toppled with tremendous circumstances as a test of our character. The true test is not the decisions you make about the given situation, but the attitude you take in how you choose to handle what you are going through, while you are going through it. Learning to trust God and lean into him for all that we are and need demonstrates our faith and increases our strength, giving us the ability to persevere. Life is a huge game of cause and effect! When you learn who you are, then you also develop a better sense of what you will and will not accept, which will impact your ability to make better choices. Our decisions, whether positive or negative will generate an outcome like it or not, and we must then deal with the reality of the decisions we make, this is how we gain life's experience.

It is through life's experiences we learn to prepare for our future. What is discouraging about this process is that it is not black and white, nor does it come with an instruction manual; life is full of many grey areas, which cause us to react and respond accordingly. Life is cultivated by uncertainty and constant change, which offers several chances if we are lucky to correct our mistakes along the way. We are all blessed with a past and a future; that's God's will. But if we take a second to stop and examine our present state, and reflect on our past, then and only then can we better prepare for the future. I have learned a great deal about myself from following this very principle. For every tomorrow there is a yesterday, which means we all have a past. Do not be afraid of what you left behind, use it as a tool to help you get where you are going. As I examined my past in all of its splendid mistakes, with a multitude of failures and disappointments, it gave me hope.

You see, life is an excellent teacher. I realized that my past did not have to dictate my future, yet it would help me to learn, grow, and move towards my destiny. This principle not only caused me to seriously think outside of the moment, but also gave me a healthier understanding of myself and who I wanted to become, not how others saw me or thought I should be. It was then that I was able to truly re-evaluate where I had been, gain knowledge and wisdom about where I was in my life, and re-aim my goals for where I intended to go. God has given me the strength to redirect my steps toward a more promising and enlightened future, full of positive changes and healthy reflection. Let the journey begin!

Chapter I: Life's journey

Life is a wakeup call

If you are the average typical person who realized early on that you were not birthed into a perfect society, and even your parents or siblings were just as imperfect and constantly gave you pause, you are not alone. *Many people meander through life thinking I wish I had different parents, I wish I were an only child or had brothers and sisters, there is always an underlying 'I wish' or 'what if' to keep our minds wondering.* The reality is you are exactly where you should be, and have been dealt the hand that God intended for your life, now it is up to you what you do with it. *"The word of the Lord came to me saying, before I formed you in the womb I knew you, and before you were born I set you apart"* (New International Version, Jeremiah 1.4-5). Regardless of how your life began, or from what lineage you derived, the promises of God are deeply imbedded within us to give us hope and the courage to seek the life he so graciously desires us to have.

Prepare to pursue life! One of my favorite quotes by McNally states "your past cannot be changed, but you can change tomorrow by your actions today" (qtd. in Hudson and McLean xx). Therefore if we view our past experiences as lessons for tomorrow, we will continue to pursue life to the fullest with passion and a purpose. Ouspensky states "It is only when we realize that life is taking us nowhere that it begins to have meaning" (qtd. in Hudson and McLean 52). The pursuit of life is probably the most ambitious way to live. This theory offers you several challenges; it encourages you to set goals and plan ahead, and to go after your dreams and never stop striving to achieve. Do we all possess the character of pursuit? No, for some the satisfaction of a children, family and running a household are pursuit enough. But understand that forward movement and the constant pursuit of "something" other than your self will ignite a certain hope and a desire to achieve more. We are taught early in life and it is declared in the constitution that we have a right to the pursuit of happiness. But each individuals happiness by their own definition and by whatever means necessary be it money;

career, love, or material things, guides us through life with a sense of hope for something better. Whatever your personal pursuit is, you can be certain that life will bring absolute and uncertain change when you least expect it, be ready to change with the rest of the world and embrace a new pursuit.

When uncertain change strikes we tend to respond on the basis of our environmental existence, what we know. If you have embraced faith as a lifestyle sudden change may be less relevant to you than that of someone who reacts with the shift of the wind. Understand that the one thing in life that is constant is change, and it will give you a new perspective on how to keep moving forward without losing momentum or hope along the way. It doesn't matter where you came from, every one of us is equipped with the God given strength to overcome life's unexpected challenges and continue to push forward. You must first have a dream and desire for something bigger than where you are now. If you have no desire to go anywhere, then it is inevitable that you will remain standing still, but with every dream that is inside of you hope will positively propel you to create a goal to help you get there.

I use to be one of those people who constantly lived in fear. I had no clear understanding or definition of my life's goals. But I always had a yearning and desire for something better than where I was in my life. This desire grew more intense as my children became a little older, and my dreams and desires for the life I wanted them to have intensified. I knew I wanted them to go to college and have successful lives. But the fact that I had not made education a priority in my own life discouraged my dreams for them. After a long talk with myself and God through constant praying I did return to school. It was one of the most frightening experiences of my life, because by then I was almost 40 years old and intimidated by the classroom, and the thought of someone else re-shaping my way of thinking. After I completed my Bachelors of Science degree in organizational management, I though ok, I did it! I'm done! After all I had achieved a tremendous personal accomplishment. But God in all his glory and with an enormous sense of humor said *"I'm not finished with you yet."* I have since earned an MBA and am currently a second year Ph.D. candidate in business management, with a specialization in management education. I am also an adjunct professor at a university, where my passion for teaching is greatly manifested. Truly God is no respecter of person and he does not show partiality, if he did it for me just image how much more he will do for you. All you need is the right wake up call! That driving force inside you that screams for you to take notice; an underlying reason or motivation to take an inventory of where you are in your life and decide where you want to go!

- *Regardless of how your life began, or from what lineage you derived, the promises of God are deeply imbedded within us to give us hope and the courage to seek the life he so graciously desires us to have.*

- *It does not matter where you came from or how your life began, focus on where you are going and how to discover your wake-up call!*

- *Whatever your personal pursuit is, you can be certain that life will bring absolute and uncertain change when you least expect it, be ready to change with the rest of the world and embrace a new pursuit.*

Life as a teacher

Knowledge is something that is acquired through life experiences and interaction with others. Formal education is not the only platform for instruction and at times the world around us is the best possible classroom. The scripture states *"my people are destroyed from lack of knowledge"* (Hos. 4.6). Learning is an ongoing and continuous cycle; everything that happens to you is your teacher. Use it to your advantage and as an opportunity to improve, rectify and re-invent yourself in his image. Berends suggests "everything that happens to you is your teacher, the secret is to learn to sit at the feet of your own life and be taught by it" (qtd. in Hudson and McLean 28). Therefore as the rules of life change, and they will, be ready to change with them.

We learn and are taught many things in life, from the basic fundamentals of survival, to human and technical skills in our work environments. Learning creates an upward progress, which enables you to prosper and grow, and if you are honest and hardworking you will undoubtedly reap the rewards of that prosperity. Most people never realize the learning opportunities that exist before them, after all a trip to the grocery store can be a learning opportunity if you view it correctly. The concept of life as a teacher becomes very clear when you begin to reflect on your goals and dreams. For it allows you a chance to take a look back at where you have been, analyze your mistakes and shortcomings, then identify with what changes and adjustments you should make to move into your new found future.

Day after day people go about their lives not realizing that today can be different then yesterday, tomorrow can be profoundly different than today! The first step toward making a change for tomorrow is realizing the need for it today. If you are stagnate, or at the crossroads of your life and have no idea what to do next stop and evaluate where you have been before deciding where you should go.

The key is to be truly honest with yourself about how much of your life you have wasted on unproductive efforts or negative strife-full attitudes that bear no fruit. It is never too late to have the life you desire. Does that mean it will be an easy adjustment? Absolutely not! The hardest part though is finally admitting to yourself that "something needs to change" that is a tough realization for most, especially if you have become accustomed to living and functioning a certain way all or most of your life, to suddenly wake up one day and say I'm going to change my life today is huge! The good news is it is possible and you have a helper, God!

Prayer and submission to God is a powerful thing. If you have never experienced the love of God through his correction, guidance and encouragement, you are in for the most influential and profound change yet! He is amazing and will take you to a place of peace like you have never before experienced.

It is easy to think we can change our behavior on our own accord, but is that realistic considering you have probably behaved the same way all of your life. Change even within our self is sometimes harder to face than what the world throws at our doorstep. Often times the initial shock of realizing that we even need to change in one aspect or another is a devastating realization. I believe the saying "you are always the last to know" applies here. In context it means something completely different; however, in theory demonstrates how little we self-evaluate our own behavior and attitudes about who we are and how we are reflected on the world around us. Knowing and doing are as they say two completely different things. We may come to know and face up to who we are, but have no clue or idea what to do to fix ourselves, or transition into who we want to become.

There are several acceptable solutions for implementing personal change; self-help books, mentors, therapy, and a change of environment are just a few. However, the most effective and long term solution is the one most overlooked, God! Whether because of unbelief, fear of having to give up something, (which you probably do not need anyway), or lack of understanding about how faith operates many people turn to alternative short term solutions. God's solutions are long term and when he fixes you he actually breaks you down (humbles), corrects what is wrong and makes you whole in every area of your life; before he restores you to the person you were created to be. God's guidance gives you a sense of purpose and direction unparalleled to anything you have ever before known. Look at the story of Jacob or David in the bible, before making them great men, God first broke them down (humbled) them in order to make them great. Spurgeon suggest whenever God is going to use you, give you an enlargement or bring you into a larger platform of spiritual life, he must first break us down in order to make us a greater sphere of usefulness (1). The concept of breaking us or humbling us is so you can see the power of God moving in your life through positive changes and developments that would not have occurred by your own hand. God wants us to recognize and acknowledge him as he re-builds us. Change takes discipline; most of us lack the discipline necessary to take on such a huge personal transition on our own. But the good news is you do not have to go it alone, God is still in control, and he will supply you with the self-control you lack to accomplish the wholeness you are missing.

Take a close inventory of your life and re-examine the areas you would like to see improve. If you have ever felt incomplete or like there was something missing in your life, maybe that's because there is, the wholeness of God! He will fill the emptiness with such harmony and balance that you will begin to see your life and the world around you in a new light. Look at what your life has taught you this far right or wrong, good or bad and use it as a textbook to study ways in which you can benefit from the past, by redefining your future and allowing life to serve as your teacher!

- *Many of life's lessons can be learned just by examining   your own life's mistakes!*

- *The opportunity for change occurs when you realize the need for it!*

- *What has your life taught you so far?*

- *Learning is an ongoing and continuous cycle; everything that happens to you is your teacher. Use it to your advantage and as an opportunity to improve, rectify and re-invent yourself in his image.*

- *RE-define your future and allow life to serve as your teacher!*

The Past does not dictate your future

Many people get stuck right where they are because they have given up hope of ever having a better life or making positive changes to their norm. We tend to fall into the "This is just my life" trap; the *trap* is it does not have to be unless that is what you choose. There are many adversities to life in which everyday people can get caught up in without warning. Whether it is alcohol or drugs, sex, or criminal behavior, excessive debt, or relationship issues you can leave your past in the past. Living an on the edge lifestyle can diminish your self-esteem and destroy your confidence to an extreme low to where you begin to accept that you are less than worthy of anyone's love, much less that of the creator of the universe.

God dealt with me on some of these issues in such an amazing way. I had no choice but to acknowledge his presence it was that strong, and in that moment of enlightenment, I knew I was not alone nor did I ever have to be again. You see, I allowed a man I loved to make me feel less than acceptable because I did not meet up to his standards and expectations of who he thought I should be. The truth is it was never about me, but moreover about his arrogant need to make a superficial impression on others. Though I was distraught at the thought that I was not good enough in his eyes, I truly thank him today for encouraging me to re-evaluate who I was and to take action toward improving some areas of my life. Without even realizing it his ostentatious comments challenged me to set some goals and pursue a different path, it was a virtuous learning experience.

We have all encountered people that challenge our sense of being in one form or another, whether it is a family member, co-worker, boss or significant other, instead of taking it personally and going on the defensive; stop, take a self-assessment and ask yourself if their comments are valid and worthy of reflection. Often times it is tough to get past the criticism, but when you do and are honest enough to acknowledge the validity of the critique, consider it free education. Not to mention thousands of dollars saved on countless hours of wasted therapy.

I also went through most of my life allowing my mother to categorize me as indifferent because I wanted more for my life. I believe at times she took it personal, as if I thought I were better than her or resented my life. However, that was never the case; I just knew for me God had a different plan and vision for my life, one I was determined to follow. When you begin to set goals you grow to expect more of yourself, and the life you were accustomed to will appear narrow in comparison to the broad views that world has to offer. This is a transitional stage where most people do not realize what you are going through or how to respond to you changing around them especially if their environment is still the same. In no way does that mean you have adapted the thought that you are better than anyone else, it simply means that in this progressive stage the measurement of your growth is that every day you become a better person than you were the day before. The reality is not that you think you are better than anyone else, but "you will strive to better than yourself." If you are willing to expand the way you think you will increase your capacity for goal achievement and ultimately personal and spiritual growth.

Do not ever allow anyone to make you compromise who you are just to satisfy their expectations of who they desire you to be. God designed you uniquely in his image, not theirs! When you lower or even raise your standards to meet the expectations of others you lose a part of yourself and become trapped in identity crises, not knowing who you are or where you fit in. Instead follow your heart, stand firm in what God has put inside of you and allow that dream and desire to lead and guide you. In doing so you remain true to yourself and God only seeking to please him, this is what we should do anyway. I would rather meet up with his expectations any day than try to please people who will come and go out of my life at a moment's notice. When people do not take the time to recognize and learn who you are from the inside out they miss out on a huge learning opportunity of their own, the chance to truly indulge in God's glorious creation, you! God has shown me how valuable and worthy I am and how his love for me is unconditional. When you know and understand this for yourself, it will further teach you how to love others in much the same way.

Be even warier of people in your immediate environment who dread the thought of you leaving them in a state of self-destruction while you try to change. I have heard so many people say I will get saved when I fix some things in my life. Hey I get it, I use to be one of them, until I realized that I could not do it on my own, nor did I have to. The scripture says come to me as you are. *"Come to me, all you who are weary and burdened, and I will give you rest. Take my yoke upon you and learn from me, for I am gentle and humble in heart, and you will find rest for your souls"* (Mt. 11.28-29).

The truth is regardless of how noble your intentions might be we cannot make that type of insurmountable change on our own. Though you may try and possibly succeed for a short period of time, life has a way of throwing curve balls at you that will send you spiraling back into your old habits faster than you can say not me! However, when you have God working in your favor, when you have submitted it all over to him, he will take away the desire and urge that you have to ever go back to the past.

Once you have relinquished the past and all of its glorious mistakes to that of experience take notes and turn it over to God, every dream you have for the future will become that much more realistic and tangible. God puts dreams and desires in all of us, which help to give us hope for what's ahead. But unfortunately we cannot by pass the present. Sorry, I did mention that we have to fix a few things first right? There are a lot of things we could probably bypass in life our current state of being is not one of them.

Change is a process, one that does not happen overnight. The funny thing is once you reach a sense of enlightenment about who you were and the things you use to do, you will want to fast forward to the future so quickly you will get a headache just trying to figure out how to make that come to pass. Slow down; just remember God is at work in your life! Our plans are not always his, and because we only see a portion of the picture we tend to miss a lot. God has the whole story from beginning to end and every spectacular detail in between. He has anticipated our ups and downs, and mapped out the best possible advantage for our success. So when (and notice I *did not* say if), but when you become discouraged because things did not work out the way you hoped or desired, remember God is still working out the kinks for a successful end. He wants to give you all the desires of your heart, and sometimes we desire a lot, which means well laid plans take time. Be patient and faithful where you are, this demonstrates to God that we trust him, in doing so he will ensure that we have an *"exceedingly and abundant life" (Eph. 3.20).*

Hofner quoted "A preoccupation with the future not only prevents us from seeing the present as it is, but often prompts us to rearrange the past" (2). We are fortunate enough to receive do overs in this life, not on everything, don't get me wrong, some mistakes we just have to choke down like a peanut butter sandwich with no milk, but that does not mean we have to allow those mistakes to define who we are. The key to rising above the mistakes of your past is to first not repeat them, and next, *learn* how to improve on them; the key word here being learn again life's best teacher is some of our worst mistakes.

For many years I struggled with low self-esteem. Those that know me personally would never know that to be the case because they viewed me differently. For all intense purposes I have been happy, outgoing, kind and pleasant on the outside, but struggling to keep a grasp on reality on the inside. You see like most women seeking the heart felt desire to be loved at all cost, typically because it was not something readily experienced in childhood. I grew up without ever knowing the love of a paternal father, and allowed myself to fall into abuse relationships, and endured men that took advantage of that need and longing for love. This is a common mistake for many women that have not yet learned to make the correlation between love and sex. Misunderstanding of what love actually is can cause you to seek affection and intimacy, instead of adoration and respect, which is what you deserve. It is only when you discover God's love that you will in turn, discover love of self. The ah ha moment is when you come to understand that there is a huge degree of separation between the two, and that one does not necessarily validate the other.

Many women have fallen into this deception for a variety of reasons, mainly because of the desire (and need) to be loved. No one wants to be alone, companionship and the thought of sharing your life with the one that will complete you are typical desires, not only for women, men seek it as well. It took many years and the help of God to realize my self-worth break the curse of abuse and learn to value myself as more than just an object. Regardless of what your struggle is adversity comes in many forms, but the realism is God will give you the strength to fight against the desire to go back to the past. *The past does not dictate your future!* Once you have conquered it and put it behind you, you will be in a better position to move into the exceeding and abundant life that God promises. You will begin to discover a supernatural strength pushing you toward your hopes and dreams for a better tomorrow, and the past will soon fade into a distant memory.

- *Once you have relinquished the past and all of its glorious mistakes to that of experience take notes.*

- *Live to meet God's expectations, not peoples!*

- *Striving to be a better you does not make you better than anyone except yourself!*

Chapter II: Knowledge and Growth

How to Learn from your past

The past should never be discounted as a shameful memory, or something so easily forgotten. I said earlier in chapter I that my past has been an excellent teacher for my future path. You see, learning from my mistakes and allowing God's correction has given me the strength to be a better mother, sister and daughter. One of the major learning milestones for me was the understanding that I did not have the capability to change anyone except myself.

Holding onto hatred and anger because of abuse or painful situations of your past hold only one purpose, they serve as painful reminders of what you cannot let go of and barriers to your future. In acknowledging this realization, I also came to realize that the only person I was hurting was me. It is true what they say about holding onto anger. While you are still mad and upset over things that other people have done to you, they have moved on in life and have no clue why you begrudge them. Meanwhile, as you continue to hold on to whatever you can't let go of, you have relinquished your power over to them. The most therapeutic moment in my life was the day that I asked God to forgive me for the hatred I felt in my heart and sought forgiveness from the people I carried those feelings for, it was truly liberating. I have never in my life felt such a sense of peace and it was as though a huge weight lifted off of me. It was in that moment that I also sought to change my own perspective, which led to healing and the victorious retrieval of the power that was previously lost.

As a mother my children are the most important people in my life after God, and I wanted to make sure to do everything possible to help them be strong, healthy and productive people in their own lives. What I came to realize in that is the beginning of this journey of motherhood began with my past and that if I did not walk away from it with my life's lessons in hand, I could potentially set my children up to face the same mistakes and shortfalls as I did. Most times we tend to fall into the belief that our mistakes aren't hurting anyone but us. This is a huge misconception, the truth is everyone around you is affected by the decisions you make, and if they have negative consequences than often times our children more so than others reap the fallout. Our children sense our fear, our anger and our emotions more so because of their proximity, but consider this without realizing it we are also indirectly teaching them our own misguided behavior. If you want your children to be respectful lead by example by respecting others; if you want your children to be forgiving lead by example by showing them forgiveness. Life's most valuable lessons are the ones we teach our children, they are after all the next generation and a true representation who we are. I thank you Lord for strengthening me to teach them the way they should go! The scripture says *"train a child in the way he should go, and when he is old he will not turn from it"* (Prov. 22.6).

Through the course of our life we can either embrace the changes that so rapidly overtake us or sit on the sidelines and let it all pass us by. If we can identify the patterns of the past, and where we are in the grand scheme of things then we can then identify the best course of action for guiding our life. The last place you want to be is stuck in a state of "stagnation" and "uncertainty." This is where you become negative and reluctant to believe for something better, which will cause you to become reactive and trapped by life's complications. As I began to examine my own life and where I was headed, I gained invaluable insight about who I did not want to be. Knowing this in turn gave me a renewed sense of energy and the ability to stay focused on where I was. When you truly reach that "go for it" stage of life where all of heaven seems to be lined up in your favor, seize the moment, forget the past and let your goals and dreams yield you into an amazing future. When you reach this phase of achievement in your life you will find that you have gained an overwhelming since of commitment to whatever you set your sights on, and you will approach it with logic, drive and the sense of purpose, which will carry you forward.

Life has a strange way of making you stand up and take notice. At some point you have to ask yourself, do I merely want to be an observer or participate in the direction in which my life is heading? This in itself will cause you to wake up and take responsibility for everything that happens in your life going forward. A quote from

Dostoyevsky states "The secret of man's being is not only to live, but to have something to live for" (qtd. in Hudson and McLean 57). Embrace wisdom, knowledge and understanding of self as a rule to live by and this will be the foundation of every goal you seek to achieve and because learning is a continuous cycle, you will always have something to live for. *"Wisdom is the principal thing; therefore get wisdom: and with all thy getting get understanding"* (Prov. 4.7).

It is often said that the reason the windshield of your car is much larger than the rear view mirror, is because where you are headed is much more important than where you have been. Learn from your past, but do not allow it to become an obstacle to your future!

- *Forgiveness releases you from bondage!*

- *The past should never be discounted as a shameful memory.*

- *Life's most valuable lessons are the ones we teach our children!*

- *Embrace wisdom, knowledge and understanding of self as a rule to live by.*

Mistakes create an opportunity for a

victorious comeback

At the age of 20 I was married and had my first child. I married straight out of high school and as for as long as I can remember my life was about taking care of someone else. I have always worked full-time and supported myself, but I cannot say that I had ever fully realized my personal dreams until my forties. I have no regrets where my children are concerned, my daughter now 25 and my son now 20 are outgoing, intelligent, educated young people with ambitions and dreams of their own.

I always thought when I turned forty that was it, I would be considered old, outdated and out of touch with everything. The irony is that it wasn't until my forties that I truly began to make the connection of life experiences to personal achievement. Like most people I closed the blinds on the past and attempted to move forward, but the problem was I repeated some of my previous mistakes, and for years seemed to travel in a vicious circle. Again, God dealt with me by showing me areas of my life that I had not fully learned from. Understanding and confessing my short-comings helped me to achieve dreams and goals I never thought possible. Getting married at such a young age to most seemed a big mistake, maybe so. But, God used my mistakes for my good. The lesson in that was that understood the need to mature and grow and learn along the way, which helped to prepare me for everything that I am experiencing now. They say wisdom comes with maturity, back then I lacked the maturity to be what God intended; now I have with greater insight, wisdom, peace, self-respect and clarity of his plan for my life. Facing challenges and difficulties of divorce and single parenthood was not always an easy, there were many times I felt I was in over my head. Whether you are a single parent or a married couple raising children life's complication are bound to come in various forms. If you allow defeat to keep you stranded in lack, chaos and stress then you have ignored one of God's most rewarding scriptures, which state "the thief comes only in order to steal and kill and destroy. I came that they may have and enjoy life, and have it in abundance to the full, till it overflows" (Jn. 10.10). God orchestrates victorious comebacks like no body's business. When you reach a point when you feel like giving up or giving in, allow God to guide you with that little voice that gently says, you are a child of the most- high God, I have a good plan for your life, one to prosper you and he will!

Every day we face difficulties that leave us drained, disillusioned and distraught over things we have gone through or may still be going through. Whether you are facing financial troubles, family issues, job loss or any other emotional trauma, remember God is in control. Now I am not one for clichés, and trust me there are many of them out there to cover a multitude of situations, but the reality and undeniable truth is in your most difficult of moments, when you think your life is over and your world is coming to an end you will discover God's amazing presence in the most unexpected way. Most people see their difficulties as a setback in their life, be it loss of material things or possessions, a break-up or divorce, job loss or even bankruptcy, and yes I used the "B" word, the reality is sometimes along the way in life we forget to seek God's guidance before jumping head first into this thing called life!

The certainty of the difficulties we face is that at some point you have to deal with the fallout. As part of a corrective *process* to get us back on track to what God has in store for us as part of his plan for our life, we have to be restored. We spend endless hours praying, begging and making promises we will never keep in hopes of getting God to move in our life and fix the problem. We get so caught up in life that we forget to seek God's wisdom before making choices and decisions that will affect the rest of our life.

The *process* is not the problem; it is part of the solution. When you stay in faith and trust God to be God, you will come to realize that what seemed like a devastating blow to your life was the best thing for you, its called correction (God's Love). What seemed like a setback was merely a set-up for God's victorious comeback. God has promised that if we diligently seek him first, he will give us the desires of our heart. *"But seek first his kingdom and his righteousness, and all these things will be given to you"* (Mat. 6.33). God's word did not suggest we go after things, then come back and ask for his advice and guidance later, hence "seek first." When we fall backward into life's problems we expect a quick, fast and in a hurry resolution to problems that we have sometimes taken a life time creating. The secret to finding strength to your victorious comeback lies in your faith and trust in the only one who can move mountains and produce miracles beyond that of your wildest imagination. The scripture tells us *"and without faith it is impossible to please God, because anyone who comes to him must believe that he exists and that he rewards those who earnestly seek him"* (Heb. 11.6).

When you rely on God, by faith knowing his word does not return void and he will do all that his word says he will do, you will begin to experience God's promises and a sense of calm and inner peace that truly surpasses all understanding. He will walk you through the process! Notice I said through, there is no getting over here you have to go through some things to be able to reflect back on his goodness and recognize his presence in your life.

- *The process of correction is not the problem; it is part of the solution. Allow him to walk you through the process!*

Learning is a never ending journey

Life presents us with the opportunity to learn every day! People will challenge you and cause you to lose your religion at the drop of a dime, and test the boundaries of your patience beyond normal limits. This is just who we are as people we were derived from sin, Adam and Eve made sure of that when they disobeyed God in the Garden of Eden. We are controversial, challenging, and indifferent human beings with the power to change someone else's entire life with the lash of our tongue. According to the scripture, *"death and life are in the power of the tongue"* (Prov. 18.21).

How you affect the lives of others begins with what you say or merely how you say it. We can find fault in everything and everyone, we are masters at judging others, but when was the last time you took a good long look at yourself. Let's just deal with that first! None of us are perfect; we have already determined that to be true, so as imperfect as we are why do we continue to hold others to higher standard of accountability?

Choose to empower someone else by speaking encouragement and positivity into their life and situation. Do not allow your current state of aggravation to turn you into someone you do not want to be, and will soon come to regret and despise every time you look in the mirror. We cannot consciously live happy and productive lives while we constantly diminish the lives of others through our careless and thoughtless acts. *"A kind man benefits himself, but a cruel man bring trouble on himself"* (Prov. 12.17). My grandmother once told me it cost you nothing to smile and be kind to someone!

Other people's discouragement and bad disposition does not have to negatively impact your behavior, does it? At times it will, we tend to allow the attitude of others to determine our own attitude, why give anyone else that kind of power over you. Sometimes, the best response is none at all. Do not allow yourself to get caught up in drama and indulge some else's need for controversy. Learn how to rise above the situation and walk away. Now you may do so thinking "I should have said this or I should have done that," but in retrospect the choice you made to rise above the situation is a healthy reflection of who you choose to be in God!

Learn to listen! We spend so much time in conversation preparing our response and comeback that we fail to hear what is actually being said. Studies show we only listen to about 20 percent of what is said; because we are too busy talking the other 80 percent (Adler and Elmhorst, 81). You actually learn more from listening than you do by talking. Think about it, you are already familiar with your own thoughts, ideas and perspectives'; listening gives you the opportunity to gain the perspective of others and examine different viewpoints. I have learned so much by just listening to other people talk. Listening may encourage an idea, confirm a thought, generate new thoughts or ideas and ultimately increase your wisdom and knowledge.

Because learning occurs in different settings in and outside of a traditional classroom the capacity to increase your knowledge is endless. Open yourself up to the endless prospects of free education, whether in the workplace, the marketplace, your community or through mass media "everyday learning" (Illeris, 35) offers the potential for continued growth and the expansion of our minds eye.

The older we get the more settled we become in who we are and that is hard to change, but not impossible. Complacency is a choice and like me, most of you resist any attempt anyone makes to impede on your way of thinking. In reality, is what you are holding onto in your mind that valuable that it makes it entirely impossible for you to tolerate a different perspective? It is true that with age comes wisdom, but it can also be said that wisdom does not automatically come with age. Wisdom is gained through experiences, interactions and listening to those that preceded you who embraced change and learning with determination and tenacity. *"The wisdom of the prudent is to give thought to their ways, but the folly of fools is deception"* (Prov. 14.8). Do not be foolish in your thinking or allow fear of learning to ground you in deception. I recently read an article about a 99 year old man in Redmond Oregon, returning to college to receive his degree from Eastern Oregon University. He dropped out of school during the depression, but found the fortitude at 99 years of age to finish what he started (Wilson). He made a choice, one to continue growing and learning as a journey. It is never too late, with the many options to formal education and learning these days, you never even have to leave your home.

Do not allow fear or complacency to keep you from achieving your dreams, and if education and the achievement of a college degree is still embedded somewhere inside of you, step out on faith and God will strengthen you in your weakness. By no means am I saying that you have to go to college to learn, you may have other untapped dreams and desires that have never been realized. Whatever those dreams are and regardless of how far-fetched they may seem rely on the strength of God to bring you to that point of fulfillment. Scripture tells us to *"fear not, for I am with you; be not dismayed, for I am your God; I will strengthen you, I will help you, I will uphold you with my righteous right hand" (Isa. 41.10).*

- *Choose to empower someone else by speaking encouragement and positivity into their life and situation.*

- *Learning is a continuous cycle.*

- *Do not allow fear or complacency to keep you from achieving your dreams!*

Life-long learning enhances your vision

Life-long learning is defined in Wikipedia as the continuous building of skills and knowledge throughout the life of an Individual. It is through experiences, life situations, education and relationships that we encounter over the course of our life that contribute to life-long learning. Life-long learning in all its significant glory has the capability to motivate your pursuit and vision regardless of what that may be. Informal and Formal education exist in different mediums and the continued acquisition of knowledge in any form should be a continuous quest.

I have personally experienced times in my life when I have wanted something so badly that I said double prayers trying to get God to respond. Regardless of what it is you are believing God for and I did not get it, do not become discouraged and give up thinking nothing good is ever going to happen for me. Just remember our plans and visions are not always what God himself intended for our lives. In the very moment you are tempted to feel discouraged, God will literally direct you toward a new vision, one that he had already pre-destined for your good. People become stuck and depressed in not receiving what they want and fail to realize that God is trying to give you the desire of your heart through a bigger and better vision. Pay attention! Oh and did I mention earlier in this book that God's vision, his plan for our life is far bigger than anything we could ever think, hope for or imagine. If God directs you toward a different dream or vision he already knows it will work out for your good, trust him!

As I previously mentioned, my decision to return to school at almost 40 years of age was a terrifying experience, but by the same token, the most gratifying one of my life! Fear will ground you and prevent you from steeping out on faith to pursue what your heart desires, but you have to be strong enough in mind to know that in your moment of weakness God will stop walking with you and he carry will you. Whatever your goal or vision put some action to it and watch it unfold into one of your most gratifying experiences. These are a few of my favorite quotes to help inspire your vision.

- *Commit yourself to lifelong learning. The most valuable asset you'll ever have is your mind and what you put into it. (Brian Tracy)*

- *Be observing constantly, stay open minded, be eager to learn and improve. (John Wooden)*

- *It is essential that along with imparting facts, that we inspire the ability and desire to learn. (Barbara Viniar)*

- *It is learning, individually and collectively, which makes us strong, gives us hope, and carries us forward. (Barbara Viniar)*

- *It is shocking to find how many people do not believe they can learn, and how many more believe learning to be difficult, every experience carries a lesson. (Frank Herbert –Dune)*

- *Learning and innovation go hand in hand; the arrogance of success is to think that what you did yesterday will be sufficient for tomorrow. (William Pollard)*

- *The man who graduates today and stops learning tomorrow is uneducated the day after. (Newton D. Baker)*

The Ability to Learn and Unlearn

Leaning, as we have already explored is the acquisition of knowledge. Just as we have the capacity to learn we also have the capacity to unlearn. You may ask why would you need to unlearn anything? Through the course of life we allow ourselves to become content and repetitious in routine to the point that we do not recognize the need to remain open minded in our thinking and ways of doing things.

When you stay open minded you essentially expose yourself up to accepting new challenges; be it skills, behaviors and of course new ways of learning. At this point you become transformed in your views and ideals. "Transformational learning is about dramatic change; fundamental change in the way we see ourselves and the world in which we live" (Merriam, Caffarella and Baumgartner, 130). Unlearning does not mean that everything you have learned this far is erased and forgotten, all it really means is that psychologically you allow yourself to examine different ways of doing and thinking, flexibility is the key.

Because we are grounded in a certain system of belief, values and cultures the foundation of everything we know is predetermined within that system of belief. Most of what we know or have been taught is generational, passed down from long line of loved ones who we learned to mimic over time, most often without even asking why? When you have been convinced that the way you think or do things is right then of course everything and everyone else will appear to be wrong. Life is full of multiple angles, and when you allow yourself to see the world through someone else's world view you begin to understand and accept the differences around you. At this point you have successfully unlearned and re-learned from a new perspective! "Learning is about more than simply acquiring new knowledge and insights; it is also crucial to unlearn old knowledge that has outlived its relevance. Thus, forgetting is probably at least as important as learning" (Blair 1).

The concept of transformational learning is not merely a technique that has to be learned for it to be beneficial in your life. The fact is it simply already exists in our daily lives, capitalizing on how to make effective use of it in your own life begins with the realization that it is possible to transform your thinking, thereby transforming your life. According to Merriam Caffarella and Baumgartner there are three stages to transformational learning; experience, critical reflection and development (144).

Experience as we have already discussed in previous chapters is critical to learning. In earlier studies of adult learning and understanding how adults learn Knowles' theoretical perspective of Andragogy details several assumptions about ways in which adults come to learn. Knowles further suggest "adults bring with them a depth and breadth of experience that can be used as a resource for their and others' learning" (qtd. in Merriam, Caffarella and Baumgartner, 144). Everything you have learned about yourself; your life, your disappointments, your tolerances and even the highlights of your life up to this point are your resources to learning. Experience gives us insight into how to successfully proceed with the rest of our lives.

Critical reflection is that ah ha moment when you pause to examine every intricate detail of your life that got you to where you are now. Good or bad, you made it through the storm and have numerous stories to share with your children and grandchildren. The ability to honestly reflect back on life's past as a lesson to be learned, analyzed and reviewed will give you insight when you least expect it. Understanding how your prior beliefs and assumptions about the world around you impacted your way of thinking, and ultimately your experiences will help you to make more sense of what you have been through and how to use it to your advantage going forward.

The third stage of transformational learning is development. "Development is the outcome of transformational and experiential learning" (Mezirow, qtd. in Merriam, Caffarella and Baumgartner 155). At some point in our lives we reach a point of enlightenment, which simply means we closely analyze our current state of being and come to examine reasoning over faith. The changes in your perspective over time will cause you to run through a gammon of emotions about whether or not God is real. Life situations come at us from all angles and so fast that it will make you ask yourself, where is God in all of this, and why isn't he here right now when I need him most? Faith is real, and it does not take a lot of it to soon realize that there is something bigger than all of us working behind the scenes of our lives. But faith is something you have to constantly hold on to, and having trust, hope and belief in the goodness of God's promise will truly help you change your outlook and maturity right where you are. Development is growth-a change of perspective about what your experiences have taught you and a healthy reflection about how to precede on a different and much more productive path.

The pivotal point of my transformational learning came after a lot of negative reflection about my life and my current state of being, which impelled me into a state of depression that I could not grasp in reality how to fix. Even though I had been saved for years and prayed often it did not seem to be enough at the time. My life had its normal ups and downs as anyone else's does I'm sure, but I had given up the optimism of ever changing my circumstances or having the life I wanted.

It wasn't until I surrendered everything I was going through to God and sought his guidance and direction for my life that I began to notice a change in my spirit. God responded to me and his message was clear and very profound, *"I'm not finished with you yet!"* Every time I felt myself losing momentum and feeling depressed, I allowed God's message to be my guide. It was soon after that that I enrolled in school and refocused my energy and direction toward wherever it was he was leading me. I learned that life's complications are a test of our faith and our ability to trust him in the midst of our troubles demonstrates the building of our character. This was a turning point in my life and in my relationship with God. I had always known he existed even from a very early age. But I can't truly say I understood what it meant to have a relationship with him. God showed me in an instance his unconditional love for me and everyday our relationship has continued to grow stronger, for me that was an amazing development.

Whatever your situation, just know you are not in it alone. God has a good plan for your life, just reflect on the road you have traveled to get where you are now and know it was not an unaccompanied journey and allow your faith to continue to guide you.

- *When you stay open minded you essentially expose yourself up to accepting new challenges; skills, behaviors and of course new ways of learning.*

Chapter III: Life is about Change

Move When the World Moves Around You!

Life is full of unexpected change good, bad or indifferent it will come. If you are someone that does not adapt well to changes in your environment be it personal, work related or in relationships this will be a difficult concept for you to embrace. However, take a close look around you. Have you noticed how different the world is today than what it was five or ten years ago? Technology in and of itself is and has become the forefront of our existence, which was not true in years past.

Everything we do today is electronically based, and if you are not somewhat technologically inclined or up on the latest technology fads or social networks you are in the minority. Long gone are the days of personal interaction and connections, even our most cherished memories captured in paper photographs are outdated and replaced by electronic media files.

The economy has left numerous people in a serious state of flux, and unless you are willing to pick yourself up and continue moving forward you will undoubtedly relinquish your dreams to that of hopelessness. The scripture says where one door closes God opens another one. Just when you are ready to give up and throw in the towel remember that he is still in control. Often times the things we hope and pray for are not part of God's plan for our lives. Do not get discouraged about closed doors, that only means that a new one is about to open up that will be more rewarding somewhere else. God is constantly orchestrating and directing our paths, and at times that will mean not allowing you to have that one thing you thought you so desperately wanted, in order to give you the fulfillment of what he intends for you to have.

God has the ability to change every situation and open new doors and windows of opportunities at a moment's notice, even when your path appears to be a dead end. Sometimes, road blocks are there to lead you unto the path Jesus would have you to go. Be encouraged and know that God does everything for a reason; not for our demise, but for our good and to His glory. The road blocks we face is simply God guiding us.

The scripture says *"everything on earth has its own time and its own season"* (Eccl. 3.1). We are not meant to remain in our same current state for indefinite periods of time. Just as God created life there is an expectation of death; just as there is light there is darkness; just as there is good, there is also the presence of evil. Forward movement is an evolutionary process, which allows us the opportunity to grow and foster new ways in which we can live, learn and exist. Resistance to change and the growth will leave you trapped in a state of stagnation and while everyone and everything else around you is moving forward you will be holding on to outdated thoughts and ideologies that have outlived their season. According to the word *"He has made everything to suit its time; moreover He has given making a sense of past and future, but no comprehension of God's work from beginning to end"* (Eccl. 3.11).

"To everything there is a season, and a time to every purpose under heaven"

A time to be born and a time to uproot;

A time to kill and a time to heal;

A time to break down and a time to build up;

A time to weep and a time to laugh;

A time for mourning and a time for dancing;

A time to scatter stones and a time to gather them;

A time to embrace and a time to abstain from embracing;

A time to seek and a time to lose;

A time to keep and a time to discard;

A time to tear and a time to mend;

A time for silence

And a time for speech;

A time to love and a time to hate;

A time for war and a time for peace"

(Eccl. 3.1-10)

Forward movement and progression are all part of God's plan for our life. Your ability to improve yourself and grow beyond your primary existence demonstrates your willingness to embrace a new perspective about change and the transition of life around you. Get out of your comfort zone and realize that just as we have environmental seasons, we also have a varied degree of individual personal seasons that bring about transition. If you are trapped by your minds view that your world is not affected by the movement of the world around you, then you have deceived yourself at a great personal cost. When you place God first in your life, diligently seeking him with obedience and faith you will see his promises begin to manifest in unexpected ways through change and growth, and new opportunities will arise that you never thought possible "open doors!"

"Moving along the upward spiral requires us to learn, commit, and do on increasingly higher planes. We deceive ourselves if we think that any one of these is sufficient. To keep progressing, we must learn, commit, and do—learn, commit, and do—and learn, commit, and do again" (Covey 306). When we commit ourselves to constant learning we are then positioned to grow and move forward without enormous effort however, if you have sold yourself an idea that you know all that you need for where you are in life, than that's probably where you will remain. Growth is a continuous educational experience, it is not something that is momentarily afforded to us as a one-time deal, it exist on a continuum in which we find strength through knowledge of self and the world around us to keeping moving forward. Move when the world moves around you!

Change is an inevitable force which cannot be stopped, derailed or interrupted by our thoughts, hopes or dreams. Even when you have become settled in your heart and mind that nothing will ever change in your life, just remember that God is still at work in your life and he has not forgotten you or the dreams that live inside you. Stay in faith knowing that in due season God will move in your life and change your whole perspective.

Allow God's words to motivate you to keep pushing forward regardless of what the enemy tries to do to get you off track. If God says *"I'm not finished with you yet"* let that be the resounding phrase that resonates through your mind every time you begin to doubt God's presence in your life, and know there is more to come. As humans living and functioning in a 'microwave" society where we have come to expect everything quick fast and in a hurry, the reality is that's not how God works in our lives. Building relationships take time, understanding God's presence and love for you through relationship enlargement is something that is cultivated over time. But the promises of God are real and when you come into relationship with him and learn to recognize his goodness in every situation of your life, you will develop a healthy praise and begin to thank him daily, even for the small things that you once took for granted. *"Delight yourself in the Lord and he will give you the desires of your heart"* (Ps. 37.4). Every morning I begin my day with a prayer of thanksgiving. I can literally look back over my life and see how God has moved and changed my perspective. I have learned to recognize his goodness and glorify him for developing me and strengthening me in areas where I did not initially see as my weaknesses. That is the glory of God, when you develop a relationship with him he will show you in no uncertain terms what areas of your life need developing. The key is to pay attention! If you are willing to allow God to move in your life then you are in for a remarkable breakthrough.

One of the most astounding stories about change that exist in the Bible is the story of Ruth and Naomi. Ruth was an ordinary woman, not seen as a great leader or prominent figure of any kind; she was just an ordinary Moabite woman. The bible tells how Ruth and Naomi were unlikely friends from different ethnic backgrounds and a generation apart. But Ruth's loyalty and love for her mother-in-law through life's unexpected change after the deaths of their husbands demonstrated an enormous strength of character in Ruth. The scripture says *"where you go I will go, and where you stay I will stay. Your people will be my people and your god will be my God. May the Lord deal with me, be it ever so severely, if anything but death separates you and me"* (Ruth 1.16-17). In essence Ruth was saying I refuse to stay down and discouraged because my circumstances have changed. As Ruth stayed faithful to Naomi and came to worship God with her loyalty to Naomi, God blessed her with Boaz. Even the worst of situations have the most promise, from God's perspective it is when we are at our worst that his blessing have the greatest impact. It is then that we can clearly see his astounding presence and in turn give him the glory he so abundantly deserves. We are designed to be a living testimony to his goodness, and we are destined to face change with every new season, just be ready to move when the world moves around you!

- *To everything there is a season!*

- *The road blocks we face is simply God guiding us.*

- *Change is an inevitable force which cannot be stopped, derailed or interrupted by our thoughts, hopes or dreams.*

Overcoming Life's Challenges

I once attended women's conference and walked away thinking, how in the world did she know what I was thinking and feeling? You see the speaker hit on some very key personal feelings and issues that I had been dealing with very privately. I had not discussed what I was feeling with anyone except God through prayer. The underlying message was about the struggle between good and evil; she began by saying mount up and take your sword with you! The message says *"the weapons of warfare are not carnal, but for the pulling down of strongholds"* (2 Cor. 10.4). As she continued I was inspired and it gave me hope, but then it became very odd as she continued in prophesy.

I was drawn in and she went on to say: "God will give you somebody to believe in you, God has selected you; You are getting ready to have a comeback; God's going to give you a plan and a strategy; He's going to tell you what to do in the ninth hour; The next set of blessings will come to you quick, it will happen suddenly, you will put your hand on it and God will manifest it; Do not become *bewildered,* learn to take God at his word; Do not become *bitter,* Trust God and keep a good attitude; What you are going through will make you *better;* You purpose has pain, and your pain builds power." As she continued her message became even more thought provoking and personal: "Before the year is out the Lord is getting ready to make an end to your enemies; And every good thing he promised you, he is getting ready to perform; Go in peace for the Lord has granted your request; The Lord said he is going to give you what you asked for; Lean not to your own understanding; A generational curse is going to turn into a generational blessing; there is something in you that's worthwhile; you may have been born from difficult circumstances; But God called you to be here; Your mother may have talked about you, you may not have known your father, but God gave you life; You can be whatever you say you can be *"so a person thinks in his heart, so is he"* (Prov. 23.7); God can use you right where you are, stop beating yourself up; God calls us to be where he wants us to be; I know the thoughts I have for you!"

Everything I had been thinking and feeling when I went into that conference was somehow secretly confronted through a women I had never before met. God used her to speak to everything that was keeping me from moving forward. I accepted her message as a challenge to let go of all of the hurt of my past and let God move in my life through the promises of his word. To this day I have witnessed his power in such amazing ways, and I have truly come to understand that with his purpose there will be pain; but as you overcome your pain you will also see an increase in your personal power, an increase in confidence, and an increase in your ability to fully trust him in every situation. As God moves in our lives he does so in levels, moving us from one degree of glory to the next. Like the shift of seasons, which we encounter in incremental proportions, experiences are gained at various levels of maturity and are such overcome through the knowledge we gain along the way.

Opposition is foundational, it exists to both challenge us and develop us in character. If you allow the weapons of warfare to succeed in breaking your spirit you will most definitely concede to defeat however, as you mount up and fight against opposition it will help to strengthen you in character and propel you into a victorious future. *"When God formed you, He placed in you all of the necessary gifting's, callings and talents you would ever need to fulfill His glorious plan for your life. He did not create you to sputter in life, stall, and fall short or to abort your mission" (Triplet 1). We were not designed to live defeated and ordinary lives; God's plan for us is much greater than what we have settled for. Life is not always fair and situations and circumstances will make you give up hope on a daily basis, but when you begin to develop an understanding and the knowledge of God's word as a blueprint for change and prosperity, you will gain the power to overcome every difficult situation that comes against you.* During the last days of His mortal ministry, Jesus said, *"these things I have spoken unto you, that in me ye might have peace. In the world ye shall have tribulation: but be of good cheer; I have overcome the world"* (Jn. 16.33).

- *Opposition is foundational, which exists to both challenge and develop us in character.*

- *We were not designed to live defeated and ordinary lives; God's plan for us is much greater than what we have settled for.*

Waiting by Faith

If you are like most patience is 'not' a virtue and waiting is just not your thing. Its ok, you're in the majority, because most of us would rather do anything other wait for something. As you are waiting to reach your next level of glory there are several key things that should help better prepare you for where God is taking you on your life's journey:

Prepare your vision and keep your mind fixed on where you are going; and serve while you wait. The best way to overcome your problems is to help someone overcome theirs; "volunteer" it will not only distract you from your own worries, but give you a new perspective into how difficult things can really be in your life. Fellowship with people who are encouraging and motivating; visit where you want to go, set your sights on the prize. Remain faithful and submissive, do all things without complaining and disagreeing; and delight yourself in the Lord "bless him at all times."

Webster's' defines faith as "*belief not based on logical proof or material evidence, belief and trust in God*" (402). Faith for most is a subjective point of view and is relative only to your personal beliefs. If you are not one that has come into agreement with how faith works, it can be as simple as belief in yourself and your ability to achieve whatever you so desire. Faith from the spiritual perspective is not a religion, but a mental acceptance of what the mind perceives and then believes as more than just a mental quality. Having faith requires a degree of trust and confidence in God that allows you to fully commit yourself to obedience. "*Faith is the substance of things hoped for and the evidence of things not seen*" (Heb. 11.1). Is this an easy concept? No! And does it take time to develop faith? Of course!

Therefore having faith means you come into agreement with the word of God for that which you have expected to manifest, and having confidence that God will act according to his word on your behalf. Faith is not a mental game of chess that we can play with God, nor is it a way to manipulate God to move in your life, it is a spiritual awareness, which grows and develops in your spirit over time and forms in your heart. The scripture says "*for with the heart one believes unto righteousness, and with the mouth confession is made unto salvation*" (Rom. 10.10). "*Without faith it is impossible to please God*" (Heb. 11:6).

Faith can increase and decrease with every evolving situation that life throws at us. Lack of faith leads to disobedience and rebellion, but having a strong foundation of trust in God regardless of what you may go through will cause him to move in your life through answered prayers, blessings and greater salvation.

There are several adversaries that deter faith: Ignorance, unbelief, fear, doubt, discouragement and self-fulfilling praise. Allowing people that lack knowledge and understanding of God's word to influence your thinking, or seeking the fulfillment of praise and approval of others over God's approval can cause your faith to decrease over-time. When we go through life grumbling and murmuring all the time, and can never find the good in anyone and anything we demonstrate a tremendous lack of faith and distrust in God.

Several years ago I was in prayer for someone who had been going through some tough trials and difficulties. After really seeking God's help to turn this persons situation around I received a revelation that truly made a lot of since. The revelation that God put in my spirit clearly said "ungrateful and unappreciative of what God has given; a husband, a job, a home, and good health, complain and gripe and God will surly take back all that he has given you." God's answer proceeded "with submit and humble your-self therefore unto the Lord, give thanks and ask for forgiveness."

The message seemed a little harsh, but was entirely true and she had allowed her circumstances to propel her into a state of doubt and hopelessness. These thoughts are typical of what many of us who are going through tough situations tend to settle into. Sharing some of our own personal revelations and experiences of murmuring and complaining can also help others to see the temporality of the situation. Examine all the great things that have happened in your life, and you will begin to see that the obstacle to your breakthrough is your inability to see the goodness of God in your circumstances. It is always easiest to blame God or the world for that matter when things are not going right in our lives. But, when you fully accept that you may have created a few of those situations along the way by manner of bad decision and choices, then you have to also accept responsibility for where you are in life and if you submit it all to God, he will give you guidance. When we take responsibility for our actions and maintain a positive attitude, we then find the ability to resist stubbornness and the pride that keeps us stuck in darkness. It is only through seeking forgiveness and acknowledging God's goodness in our life that we move closer to the light and the promises of God.

I have been in leadership positions all of my adult life and time and time again I hear people make excuse after excuse for lack of productivity or job performance. The most popular school of thought is that it is "some else's fault" that I am not succeeding! No one but you and God hold the key to your destiny, it's what you chose to do with it that determines where you will go in life and how you will get there. Take responsibility for where you are, who you are, and where you desire to be. We do not honor God with excuses and grumbling about what we are going through, we honor him through thanksgiving and praise. Doing so will move you out of your bad situation quicker and with more prosperous results than you ever though possible.

In 2003 I went through a year of dealing with crippling pain and unexplained diagnosis from doctors who constantly told me that there was nothing wrong with me. In that year I must have seen over a dozen doctors whose typical solution consisted of heavy pain medication and rest, and because they could not find any problems in the x-rays then the assumptions was there was nothing wrong with me. One Genius even told me to do leg and butt exercises to strengthen my back. The pain was excruciating and so intense I could barely walk at times. I finally saw a doctor who took me seriously and decided to do an MRI and found that I had a bulging disc in my lower back that was pressing against my spine; I had surgery a week later. I was somewhat afraid of the implications of a major surgery like that and even more afraid of living the rest of my life in pain and defeated. The operation went well and I spent four months in bed recovering. I was placed in a situation where I had no other choice but to wait, hope and believe in the promise of God for healing and restoration.

I have also had pneumonia twice; in 2006 I was hospitalized and put on bed rest for four months to recover. Again I had no choice but to wait and trust God, but this time I did something different than before I studied, prayed, read the bible and used that time to develop a deeper relationship with God. It was almost as if God said "I tried to get your attention before, so let's try that again." The Bible says "if *my people who are called by my name will humble themselves, and pray and seek my face, and turn from their wicked ways, then I will hear from heaven, and will forgive their sin and heal their land*" (2 Chr. 7.14).

God will find ways to humble you so that he can get your attention focused on him. When we do not stop to acknowledge him in all that we do and seek him for guidance we fail to experience his love and mercy in greater ways. Waiting and being patient are not easy concepts, but are necessary for spiritual growth and developing a closer relationship with God. Today I am completely healed and more active then I have ever been. I could have given in to defeat and become weary over what I was going through, but it was my faith and trust in God that gave me the strength to believe in and wait on his grace to restore me. What I learned in this experience is that your belief demonstrates a measure of faith however, if you do not put it into action, your faith alone will not cause God to move in your circumstance. *"Examine yourselves to see whether you are in the faith; test yourselves"* (2 Cor. 13.5).

My faith has generously increased over the years. I feel as though I have watched the pages of my life unfold literally before my eyes. It is almost as if someone handed me a blank book and said "here, write yourself a new chapter." The new chapter of blessings God imposed in my life has sparked a new passion for learning and growing at even higher levels. It also ignited an overwhelming desire to teach and inspire others in the way my Lord and Savior has taught and inspired me. I am no religious fanatic by any means; however, I am someone that came into the knowledge and understanding of God through reading, prayer, supplication and thanksgiving!

A true person of faith seeks to really know God through prayer, meditation and reading the Bible. However, the scripture tells us that *faith without works is dead*! If we fail to use what we learn through studying the word of God to make improvements in our life, then we are not fully living up to the potential that God put inside of each of us and we fall short of his plan for our lives. My faith has given me a sense of fulfillment and wholeness about who I am and God's good plan for my existence. I can't wait to see what he has in store for me next, but regardless of what that may be, I will continue to *wait by faith*!

- *Prepare your vision and keep your mind fixed on where you are going; and serve while you wait.*

- *When we go through life grumbling and murmuring all the time, and can never find the good in anyone and anything we demonstrate a tremendous lack of faith and distrust in God.*

- *God will find ways to humble you so that he can get your attention focused on him.*

- *Waiting and being patient are not easy concepts, but are necessary for spiritual growth and developing a closer relationship with God.*

- *Belief demonstrates a measure of faith; however, if you do not put it into action, your faith alone will not cause God to move in your circumstance.*

Chapter IV: Life Convoy

People and Choices

The quality of people we keep in and around our life are just as important as our decisions and can affect the direction our lives will take. Have you stopped to think about the people that are currently in your life? Are they adding value to you or are they dragging you down with them? Like it or not, we are most commonly influenced by the people closest to us, right or wrong we desire acceptance at such a high cost. Not everyone has your best interest at heart; even the people who you have deemed your best friends are often times secretly hoping you will fall on your face because of jealousy, envy or spite. When you take a moment to inventory your friend Poole ask yourself, if the people you are closest to positively influence your decisions? Do they share the same interest and goals? Will they praise your successes and support your failures? Do you have to change any part of who you are to befriend them? There should be no conditional expectations from the people you call your friend. Friendships are unique in that you share a bond, usually by commonality or similarities in perspectives, from this we grow together in love, trust, commitment and loyalty. When these bonds are broken we can become devastated in spirit.

Earlier in the book I discussed seasons and how our life transitions in these seasons. By the same token some friendships are only meant for a season, and it is in those seasons that either you were meant to learn something from the person you interfaced with or vice versa; they were meant to learn from you, whatever the case not every friendship is designed to be a lifelong journey. The people that genuinely love and respect you for who you are as a person, not who they can transform you into, will undoubtedly remain in your life indefinitely. Unconditional love expects nothing and asks nothing in return except that you are your best and find happiness in whatever your heart desires.

"Two people are better off than one, for they can help each other succeed. If one person falls, the other can reach out and help. But

someone who falls alone is in real trouble. Likewise, two people lying close together can keep each other warm. But how can one be warm alone? A person standing alone can be attacked and defeated, but two can stand back-to-back and conquer. Three are even better, for a triple-braided cord is not easily broken" (Eccl. 4.9-12).

God wants us to fellowship and build relationships and alliances, for the good of our development. But, just know that sometimes you have to walk away from the people you love the most in order to be the best you that God created you to be. Unintentionally or not people tend to hold us back from moving forward. We become complacent with other people that are complacent. That is not a good combination if you are a goal oriented person looking to improve some areas of your life. How can you expand and grow if you do not explore the world around you. When you open yourself up to discover new people, places and experiences, you will discover your ability to make better choices and decisions about the people you allow to influence your life and it will change you for the better.

The bible tells us that we should choose our friends wisely. How can you become wise if you are not in the company of wise men? *"The righteous should Choose His Friends Carefully, for the way of the wicked leads them astray"* (Prov. 12.26). Once you have come into agreement with God about your life and the direction you are headed, one of the things that will become most obvious is your friend Poole. When you surrender it all to God and decide to take a more righteous path, he will begin to weed out people in your life that are not moving in the same direction. Others will drop off on their own accord because it is hard for most people to grasp such a serious commitment, especially those that have no real commitments even to themselves. The scripture tells us that *"we are transformed by the renewing of our minds!"* When you are in God's hands and he is at work in you through transformation, his goal is simple to make you over in his image, into the person he wants you to become. But, if your thoughts are negatively influenced, if your hopes and desires are not set on him, then your spiritual growth and maturity is blocked and God cannot position you for his plan for your life.

As God prunes people out, he also re-connects you with others that are best suited for you at your current level of spiritual development with Him. Let him guide you to the ones that he will want you to connect with. God miraculously orchestrates the time, place and people that he desires us to meet and come into relationship with, it is an incredibility maneuvered chess move, as most of these people will be total strangers to you until God moves in to match the two of you up to satisfy his purpose. When you are moving in the path of righteousness having other people in your company that are coming into the same knowledge and understanding will lend support and encouragement. Learning is increased by listening to wise counsel, and if you cease to listen to wise counsel you will start to stray from being able to acquire more knowledge in God. The Bible says *"For the lack of guidance a nation falls, but many advisers make victory sure"* (Prov. 11.14). The scripture tells us that "evil company corrupts good habits" (1 Cor. 15.33). This does not mean that all people are bad, it just means that if your desires are to pursue the promises of God then you may want to consider who is traveling with you.

When Jesus first started to send the 12 apostles out to walk with His anointing, He would always send them out two-by-two. Once you enter into a real supernatural walk with the Lord, you will go insane if you do not have someone to share your walk with. There are simply too many good God things that will start to happen in your life, and you will need others to talk with, to vent with, to share with, to learn from one another and to help keep each other on track. Here are a few versus to help you stay focused on the journey:

- *"Do not be unequally yoked together with unbelievers. For what fellowship has righteousness with lawlessness? And what communion has light with darkness? And what accord has Christ with Belial? Or what part has a believer with an unbeliever? And what agreement has the temple of God with idols? For you are the temple of the living God"* (2 Cor. 6.14).

- *"He who walks with wise men will be wise, but the companion of fools will be destroyed" (Prov. 13.20).*

- *"A scoffer seeks wisdom and does not find it, but knowledge is easy to him who understands. Go from the presence of a foolish man, when you do not perceive in him the lips of knowledge" (Prov. 14.6).*

- *"Do not be deceived: "Evil Company corrupts good habits." Awake to righteousness, and do not sin; for some do not have the knowledge of God" (1 Cor. 15.33).*

The road less traveled!

There comes a point in our lives when we begin to examine the overall quality of our existence and question whether we are living up to our full potential. I have often heard many people ask is this all there is for me. Is this all I am meant to do with my life? We spend so much of our life bandaging up the bumps and bruises from the falls we endure and from the choices and decision we make, that we oftentimes forget that we have a helper who wants better for us than we most times expect for ourselves. Most of us feel a sense of fulfillment in having power over our life and choices, but can become powerless at any given moment by a shift in circumstances.

My belief is that fear oftentimes keeps us from seeking salvation! We are afraid of what we may have to give up or sacrifice and when you give power and control over to some else, even God the uncertainty in where you're headed can intensity your fears times ten. The road less traveled is the one that leads us on a mysterious path toward the promises of God. But when you relinquish it all over to him and learn to trust him in every aspect of your life, you will come to learn that the road less traveled is paved with eternal blessings. Will it be an easy journey? No, but well worth the trip!

It is easier to do the wrong thing or typically that which fells most comfortable to us then to what is right. The world has evolved by enormous proportions, modern conveniences, technology and constant rushing about has driven us as society to ignore traditional values like simple common courtesy. It still gets under my skin when people literally walk over me and do not bother to say excuse me, even a trip to the supermarket can be a challenge. And when did pedestrian crossing become a hazardous contact sport? Are we in that much of rush that we cannot spare two extra minutes out of our day to give the right of way to others, really? We have become such an uncaring, self-absorbed people and that is because we are moving away from the will of God instead of toward him. We are all equipped with a conscience and an inner voice that speaks to our sense of right and wrong. You know the one, the one we often ignore that ultimately screams at us from the inside out when we are about to make a bad decision.

Adhering to the word of God is about obedience. God has given us his own book (The Bible) to educate, inspire and motivate us never to live *out of* our full potential. It tells us who God is, and what God is doing and will do. As a book of prophecies and promises it reveals God's purposes and it tells us what we ought to do in order to please God. (Deut. 30.1-10) tells us of God's compassion for us and how he wants to bless and prosper us in everything we do when we obey him. Many times we ignore the inner voice that gently guides us. At times I have thought my mind was playing tricks on me, or that my own conscience was speaking to me about certain things and I brushed it off as paranoia. But just as we are guided by our conscience, we are guided by intuition and an inner spirit which communicates with us through our thoughts, feelings and environment. The inner voice or inner spirit constantly speaks to us and is meant to guide us in making better choices and decisions for our lives. Learn to tap into the voice of God and gain a better understanding of his direction and plan for your life by meditating on his word. When you began to get a better understanding of the scripture, then you will begin to recognize that inner voice as not just an overactive mind, but that of guidance and direction.

Habakkuk knew the sound of God speaking to him, when the Lord replied "*Write down the revelation and make it plain on tablets so that a messenger may run with it*" (Hab. 2.2). Elijah described it as a *still, small voice,* in which God directed him to go back the way he came "*and go to the Desert Damascus*" (I Kings 19.12). I had always listened for an inner audible voice; I thought I would immediately recognize God speaking to me. But God does not speak that way at times, nor will he speak to you in complete thoughts. I have at time been awakened from my sleep with such a strong thought that I was moved me to get up and write it down. When I examined these thoughts the next day I noticed that they were phrases, or revelations that I sometimes had no understanding of until years later.

God's voice comes as spontaneous thoughts, visions, feelings, or impressions and if you want to tap into those thoughts on a deeper level, write it down. As you began to keep journals of revelation-al thoughts by dating them and referencing them at later times, you will begin to notice a pattern that will give you direction and a sense of purpose. God has always spoken through dreams and visions, and He specifically said that" *they would come to those upon whom the Holy Spirit is poured out"* (Acts 2.1-4, 17).

In the great commission God instructs his disciples to go out into the world and teach the gospel. That is what God wants of us, to be living examples that we might glorify him by teaching others to obey his commandments not so much by what we say, but in what we do. Life's experiences and the lessons we learn from them will truly humble you and bring you into closer relationship with God and a place of peace that is indescribable. I am not a minister, nor do I claim to hold any spiritual powers that give me greater insight than that of any other person. However, what I have learned through my own experiences is this the love of God, the voice of God and his presence is real and when your faith begins to flourish you will also discover your purpose and a peace that surpasses all understanding.

Obeying the word of God will help you find peace in even the everyday menial things. Like most people I use to spend a lot of wasted time and energy grumbling about one thing or another, mostly work and the aggravations of intolerant supervisors or dealing with unhappy and rude people. But I began to thank God every day for having a job to go to and in doing that my perspective changed. I began to strive to be my best and do my best regardless of who I came in contact with. I accepted that if God placed me in this position it was for a reason, one which I may not fully understand now, but whatever the reason I know I am working to please him, which gives me peace and joy and allows me to go through my day without complaining. That does not mean I have not made the bathroom my personal prayer closet. There have been moments when I have had to retreat for a moment of silence to get past the "aggravations" but it allowed me to keep my perspective and remain professional.

God did not say he would take away every enemy and obstacle however, he does promise to make you enemies your footstool, and that no weapons formed against you shall prosper. Stay in faith and keep a good attitude regardless of where you are or what you are doing, God can use you right where you are.

When you learn to stand in faith you begin to realize that either God is strengthening you in character, preparing you for something greater, or he is using you to be a blessing to someone else. You are truly part of his purpose and plan. *"Delight yourself in the Lord and he will give you the desires of your heart"* (Ps. 37.4).When you offer up thanksgiving and praise to the Lord instead of complaining, regardless of where you are in life or what your circumstances may be, you are thereby delighting yourself in him. I often prayed and wished I was in a different career field. Management can be very challenging if you do not have the right people skills and tolerance for people in general. But I came to realize that God has kept me in the position he desired for me to be in, in order to strengthen me in character; increase my training and teaching skills and mature me for the next level in which he has prepared for me. When you align yourself with the will of God he will place you in a position of advantage and prosperity and you will soon forget about where you thought you wanted to be and learn to trust him right where you are. I never would have imagined I would be the author of a book or teaching, which was definitely not part of my plan. God knows our beginning from our end, he has purposed to give us the deepest desires of our heart and it does not always manifest in the ways we expect to see it, but it does manifest and in a much more magnificent and glorious way. He is slowly grooming me for my new career (*answered prayer*) and I know he is not "finished with me yet!" *Thanksgiving and praise demonstrates your faith and trust in him. Instead of complaining today give him Thanks!*

Obedience produces abundance and prosperity. If you truly want to see positive changes in your life change your perspective in how you acknowledge, seek and obey the word of God. My biggest challenge to understanding this was my fear that I could never live up to all the expectations of obeying the Ten Commandments, really! When I first began to actually study the bible and read it daily, I thought "I can't do this there are too many rules, and I am too imperfect." Then I read something that changed my perspective, the Bible speaks about the greatest gift of all, Love. The scripture tells us "*above all, love each other deeply, because love covers over a multitude of sins*" (1 Pet. 4.8).

Reading this scripture was a great starting point for me because I knew that regardless of anything I had been through or how I felt about my life's experiences and disappointments that I still had a strong capacity and desire to love and be loved. God had already dealt with me about forgiveness so I used that as a caveat to begin to walk in love. When I stopped expecting people to act or think as I thought they should, I began to accept people in an unconditional manner, which took the pressure off of me and them. At times I thought I was too flexible, but the reality is you cannot change anyone except yourself and if you do not like the present company then you have the option to gracefully walk away.

Love people for who they are, not what they can do for you. My conclusion in all of this was that even if I drop the ball in living up to Gods expectation (rules) of the Ten Commandments, as long as I consistently walk in Love then eventually I would learn to be more obedient in every area of my life.

"Love is patient, love is kind. It does not envy, it does not boast, it is not proud. ⁵ It does not dishonor others, it is not self-seeking, it is not easily angered, it keeps no record of wrongs. ⁶ Love does not delight in evil but rejoices with the truth. ⁷ It always protects, always trusts, always hopes, and always perseveres.

⁸ Love never fails. But where there are prophecies, they will cease; where there are tongues, they will be stilled; where there is knowledge, it will pass away. ⁹ For we know in part and we prophesy in part, ¹⁰ but when completeness comes, what is in part disappears. ¹¹ When I was a child, I talked like a child; I thought like a child, I reasoned like a child. When I became a man, I put the ways of childhood behind me. ¹² For now we see only a reflection as in a mirror; then we shall see face to face. Now I know in part; then I shall know fully, even as I am fully known.

[13] *And now these three remain: faith, hope and love. But the greatest of these is love" (1 Cor. 13.4-13). .*

Your prosperity is in your obedience! You have a choice in helping to determine your destiny. You can choose to either live a mediocre "just enough" life; you can choose to live and relive out your failures by repeating bad mistakes; or you can choose to live a life of greatness filled with victory, blessings and the promises and success of God. Your attitude and praise will determine your destiny. Step out of that negative, defeated mindset that has kept you trapped and alienated from the will of God. Instead, step into your destiny the one God desires for us that is filled with his goodness and a glorious path of victory; this is too often the *road less traveled!*

- *The road less traveled is paved with eternal blessings!*

- *Obedience produces abundance and prosperity.*

- *Love people for who they are not what you expect them to be.*

- *Your attitude and praise will determine your destiny.*

Transition: Stages of Spiritual development

As believers we are tempted and tested to prove our faith by action. Demonstrating your belief in God is more than a profession of faith, it is demonstrated in the way you live and treat people along the way. I have often heard various preachers ask through sermons "are you a partaker or a doer of the word?" I never quite got it, not right away at least. I always believed that as long as I believed and had some degree of faith that, that would be enough. But the truth is God requires more of us than that and in order to live within the will of God we must put our faith into action. Are you merely someone that attends church, takes a few notes, maybe even studies the bible in your spare time; and you can even whip out just the right verse to suit your purpose as a defensive weapon against the enemy? Or, are you someone who diligently studies, analyzes and uses scripture verses as a means of changing and improving areas of your life and to help guide others for better? If you fall into the first category consider yourself a *partaker* of the word, but if you have found enlightenment and can be grouped into the ladder category you may be called a *doer* of the word.

It took me quite some time to fall into the realization of a doer. It is always easiest to find fault with everyone else, not taking responsibility for our own actions. As a true believer and someone seeking to please God, it is our actions that demonstrate who we are and how we represent God. I have crossed paths with many people that say one thing and act completely opposite. People should be able to recognize that you are believer or that you subscribe to some form of conviction by your presence, your demeanor and your attitude. If you have to make a point of letting others know you are saved then is it really reflecting positively in your daily walk? Salvation is not a pledge that you take to get you in good with the man upstairs. Salvation is a commitment, a step toward repentance of sin and deliverance from anything that separates you from the will of God. What I gained from listening to people that proclaim to be holy, then demonstrate anything but is that we as people in general do not often times recognize our own faults and short comings. Until you either come across someone who will be more than willing to set you straight, or do some deep soul searching your actions will often times never line up with your words. The problem with this is you cannot grow or change until you realize that you need to. Sometimes you actually have to be open to complete honesty and constructive criticism about how others perceive you. You may never see things the way they do, but the saying "you will never know until someone tells you" applies here.

It is very easy to become complacent and accept that we just "are who we are" and that's all well and fine if you have no desire to ever be anything else. But because change is constant and will demand that you adjustment some part of your life at any given moment to accommodate it, it is essential to your existence that you learn to recognize areas of your being that could use minor improvements.

The simplest and yet most thought provoking concept that I adopted several years ago is that one of my personal goals is to be better than I was the year before. Now to some this may seem a bit aggressive, but it's really not it is actually a driving force that keeps me pushing to be a better me! If and when you begin to recognize certain things about yourself that you would like to see changed than that should be the foundation of your personal goals, start there. Most people set unattainable and unrealistic goals that are often times so far-fetched that you end up giving up on ever achieving them. Being a millionaire at 30 is a wonderful dream, but if you have not taken the necessary steps to achieve such success, then how attainable is it in the natural sense? I am a goal setter and I generally set 1, 3 and 5 year goals. Setting short term goals help you to constantly take a self-assessment of who you are, and who you want to become. I examine my personal appearance, my beliefs and values, my relationship with others and God, then use my findings to set short term personal goals to implement change. The 3 to 5 year long-term goals identify where you are in the grand scheme of life and help determine how you will get there. If you are a partaker, who has not yet come into a full relationship and understanding of who God is and how your actions affect your walk with him, now would be a good time to take a self-assessment and set some personal goals of your own.

As a Believer it is inevitable that you will fall into doubt from time to time. The pressures of life and stress of trying to hold it all together will absolutely make you question whether or not God is real. Rationalization of your circumstances will cause you to speculate, question and even doubt his presence. If your faith is not firmly planted you will waver between the reality of what you see happening around you (your circumstances) and what you believe to be real. Doubt will take root and may cause you to easily reject the reality of God's existence. However, if you are firmly planted in faith, though it may be difficult to do when you are going through hard times you will stand in the belief that he is real and that what you are going through is momentary and will pass. The Bible says *"My grace is sufficient for you, for my power (strength) is made perfect in (our) weakness"* (2 Cor. 12.9).

When we become weak and discouraged in the midst of our troubles the word of God promises that his strength will take over to get you through to a victorious end. If within your heart you believe that God is real, than accept his word also as reality that there is promise in every situation. Stop rationalizing your circumstances to help you make sense of the world around you because most times it never will. Instead find a bible verse that supports what you are going through and meditate on it until you have the victory God promises. *"Trust in the Lord with all your heart and lean not on your own understanding; in all your ways submit to him, and he will make your paths straight"* (Prov. 3.5-6).

Webster's defines Meditation as "an act of meditating, pondering on; a devotional exercise of contemplation" (680). If you have often wondered how to believe and trust in God in the natural realm, meditation and understanding of the word will help develop your faith. For every trial, trouble and situation we face God has already worked out a solution. Is this an instantaneous or automatic process? *No, Absolutely Not!* But meditating on the word of God will help to increase your faith, your strength and overall your ability to get through situations with the right perspective until God moves you out of whatever it is you are going through. Meditating is merely praying, reciting, and focusing your attention on God instead of the problem. This strategy has been instrumental in changing not only my perspective, but my life. As my desire to understand and have a better relationship with God increased, I did what I am suggesting to you, I began to meditate. For every circumstance or situation that I wanted to see change or improve in my life, I wrote it down along with a scripture from the bible that supported my situation. After doing this for several years I began to relinquish all of myself to improvement, because as my faith increased my desire to please God and be more like him also increased. The bible is truly our manual, a guide to self- improvement and redemption.

One of most profound examples of meditation and faith that I will share with you was one of constant plea and prayer that God would direct my path and show me my purpose. For so long I was discouraged and felt empty and lost because I felt I had no true purpose or definitive direction in my life. I found a scripture on wisdom and guidance that I used to help direct me toward God's plan for me. The Bible says "*if any of you lacks wisdom, he should ask God who gives generously to all without finding fault, and it will be given to him*" (James 1.5). I found that as I meditated and prayed on this daily that my outlook began to change and it gave me hope that I actually had a purpose first, but secondly I began to get revelation about the direction my life was taking and confirmation that God truly was directing my path. God began to open doors and move me into more instructional and teaching positions, again not my plan but his. The plans and path I had I assure you did not involve teaching, that is how I know that his plan is at work in my life, but the reality is I love it and would not want to do anything else.

As I said in the previous chapter God will speak to you in your thoughts, in your sleep, and most emphatically in your heart. But what that also showed me was that God didn't just out of the blue come up with a plan for me, it was intricately woven into his plan and purpose for my life as part of my destiny. When I look back over the last 5 years, it all makes sense and I can identify areas of my life where God has corrected me, guided and directed me, challenged me, and molded me through meditation to ultimately set me up to be the person he designed me to be. God has a blueprint for each of us that he has designed especially for you to have the happiness and fulfillment you desire. Because we take so many wrong turns on the way to redemption, he has to do a lot of clean-up work in order to make our crooked paths straight, and put us back on the right road to the fulfillment of our purpose. I know he is still at work in me (I am a work in progress) and I am very excited about what is ahead, and I Know *he is not finished with me yet!*

Allow your belief to ignite your faith in a new way. Use your bible not just as a supernatural weapon to hurl at the enemy at your convenience, but as manual for success and a guide to the transformation of a better you. Remember you cannot change anyone but you! Regardless of how many bible verses you throw at someone if they are not yet willing to come into agreement with the word of God as truth, then nothing you can say will change that. However, focus on your own walk, and how to *show* others how the word of God can transform them into a place of peace, and then you may get their attention.

People in general do not want to be preached to about what it is you think they are doing wrong. People desire the freedom to live as they choose good or bad, right or wrong. If you constantly tell them what they should change you then become the target of judgment and ridicule or just another person that thinks they are better than. But when you walk the talk, showing yourself to be upright and sincere in your attitude toward salvation then people tend to pay more attention. The basic rule is people identify with what they see, more so than what we say!

God has not asked us to be anyone other than what he created us to be. We are all uniquely and incredibly made in his image, but what he does require is that we walk in love and righteousness (morally right and just). He has not demanded perfection of any of us, only to be the best at who we are through Christ. *"And we all, with unveiled face, beholding the glory of the Lord, are being transformed into the same image from one degree of glory to another; For this comes from the Lord who is the Spirit"* (2 Cor. 3.18)

Spiritual development is not a concise scientific process, it is about discovery of who you are and the enlightenment of your inner being. As you grow through self-awareness, acknowledgement, and mediation on the word of God your inner man will cause you to take a closer look at your values, ideas and moral compass. You will come to expect more of yourself; and your abilities to change and improve through your actions and your spiritual walk will have a profound influence on others.

- *Are you are partaker or a doer of the word of God?*

- *Salvation is not a pledge that you take to get you in good with the man upstairs.*

- *Meditating is merely praying, reciting, and focusing your attention on God instead of the problem.*

- *Use your bible not just as a supernatural weapon to hurl at the enemy at your convenience, but as manual for success and a guide to the transformation of a better you.*

- *Spiritual development is not a concise scientific process, it is about discovery of who you are and the enlightenment of your inner being.*

Discovering your purpose

Your ability to understand your purpose first begins with the belief that you have a purpose. Your purpose is not merely identified by what you do (your job, your title, your address); however, it is the realization of your being, your reason for existing. Some people have settled into the mindset that allows you to merely "survive in order to exist." If you have accepted this doctrine as your own reality than you have given up on the promises of God, or could it be that you never understood them anyway? The scripture says we must die to self. What does that truly mean? To die to self simply means you have accepted the will of God for your life, which requires transformation of who we currently are in the spiritual. If God created us uniquely in his image why do we need do die within ourselves?

The process of dying to self is one of humility, strengthening of faith and transformation. It involves purging our old thoughts and ways thinking, of selfishness, pride, self-will and anything else that causes us to put self-first and God second (Eilers). Dying to self is not a physical manifestation of death, but a spiritual death that allows for a re-birth of knowledge and wisdom through the word of God. In order to be made over and molded into his image we have to first be willing to give up certain aspects of ourselves and accept a spiritual makeover. *"Then said Jesus unto his disciples, If any man will come after me, let him deny himself, and take up his cross, and follow me. For whosoever will save his life shall lose it: and whosoever will lose his life for my sake shall find it"* (Mt. 16.24-25).

The scripture also says that we should be transformed by the renewing of our mind. Does that mean we are not to think for ourselves? Renewing your mind is the acceptance of a new way of thinking, one that is more positive, encouraging and lines up with the will of God. Life at one time or another will challenge every aspect of self-discipline you have. Because we can become jaded and defensive to the ways of the world over time our attitudes, goals and ideas diminish along with our hopes. Renewing your mind is a way to re-adjust your thoughts and ideas, and challenge what you know by allowing for a new mindset. When you accept the salvation of God you are reborn, the scripture tells us "we become a new creature in Christ." If we are then reborn, but our thoughts remain the same we cannot fully manifest the transformation of rebirth that God has intended. The scripture tells us what we must do after we become born again believers. *"I beseech you therefore, brethren, by the mercies of God, that you present your bodies a living sacrifice, holy and acceptable to God. And do not be conformed to this world, but be transformed by the renewing of your mind, that you may prove to be what is good and acceptable and perfect in the will of God"* (Rom. 12.1-2).

Dying to self and renewing of the mind are transformative processes to help God develop us in character, and gently ease us into submission of his will. Once he has your full attention and your thoughts are centered on him, then he will begin to direct your steps according to his purpose for your life. Salvation is not a mandatory process it is a choice. You are also entitled to live, think and act by your own accord, but understanding the salvation of God and his purpose requires that we relinquish the mental sense of our existence to that of a new spiritual mindset, and this is when God shows up in greater ways.

Do not allow pride, arrogance or fear to keep you trapped in a destructive mindset. God has given us every provision to help us transform our thoughts to a place of peace. Start renewing your mind today by seeking the word of God for direction and discovery of your purpose. Here are a few bible verses to help you get started:

Renewing Your Mind!

Romans 1:28 - "a depraved mind, to do things which are not"

Romans 8:5, 7 - "mind set on the flesh"

Romans 12:16 - "haughty in mind"

II Corinthians 4:4 - "blinded the minds of unbelieving"

II Corinthians 11:3 - "minds led astray from simplicity"

Ephesians 2:3 - "the desires of the flesh and of the mind"

Ephesians 4:17 - "the futility of their mind"

Philippians 3:19 - "set their minds on earthly things"

Colossians 1:21 - "alienated and hostile in mind"

Colossians 2:18 - "inflated without cause by a fleshly mind"

Titus 1:15 - "their mind and their conscience are defiled"

Colossians 3:10 - "the new man is being renewed to a true"

Isaiah 26:3 - "the steadfast of mind Thou wilt keep"

Jeremiah 17:10 - "I, the Lord, search the heart, I test"

Jeremiah 20:12 - "The Lord who sees the mind and the heart"

Matthew 22:37 - "Love the Lord with all your heart, soul"

- *Renewing your mind is the acceptance of a new way of thinking, one that is more positive, encouraging and lines up with the will of God!*

Chapter V: Faith restores vision

Purpose to move forward

Have you ever heard the saying "the road to hell is paved with good intentions?" What this essentially means is that we are filled with good intent and often times mean to do well, but either end up doing bad unintentionally, or we take no action at all. There is no value in simply planning to do good if you don't actually do it. Plans are great, but actions gives momentum to our plans and thrust us toward our vision.

For the most part I do not believe we intentionally set out to fail. Life in all its glory sometimes decides those things for us. But if you have a vision, regardless of what it is put it into action and watch how it will unfold before your eyes. Fear is a powerful deterrent to the fulfillment of our visions, it often times speaks to us like a nagging little voice that just will not go away. Fear thrives on our weaknesses and tells you that you are not capable, you do not have what it takes and no one will care or support what you are doing. Do not believe the devils lies his goal is to speak enough negativity into you to make you quite before you even get started. If you have a vision that you have handed over to fear, go back and get it! You are a child of the "most-high" God and the scripture tells us "we can do all things through Christ who strengthens us." Allow your faith in the word of God to take root, restore your vision and give you a sense of purpose to move forward.

Whenever you think your life does not meet up to your expectations or you become depressed or discouraged by your own circumstances, consider that someone else somewhere is going through something far worse than you could ever imagine. We are designed to be a blessing to others, sometimes giving attentions to someone else will help you focus less on your own issues. Williamson suggests "shifts in thinking from fear to love make all the difference in how we live and how we feel; learning to think differently to stand psychologically and emotionally on a different ground of being is the spiritual journey from anxiety to inner peace" (190-191).

"Our deepest fear is not that we are inadequate. Our deepest fear is that we are powerful beyond measure. It is our light, not our darkness that most frightens us. Your playing small does not serve the world.

There is nothing enlightened about shrinking so that other people won't feel insecure around you. We were all meant to shine, as children do. It's not just in some of us; it's in everyone. As we let our own light shine, we unconsciously give other people permission to do the same as we are liberated from our own fear, our presence automatically liberates others" (Williamson 190-191).

One of the biggest obstacles to moving forward is un-forgiveness. Un-forgiveness is like an anchor tied to your ankle that will not allow you to take another step until you release it. The Bible says *"for if you forgive men when they sin against you, your heavenly Father will also forgive you. But if you do not forgive men their sins, your Father will not forgive your sins"* (Mt. 6.14-15).

Forgiveness is a powerful device; it actually has the power to grant freedom to anyone that releases it, and to oppress those that do not. When you go through life angry and tormented about the things of your past, or the people that hurt you and never acknowledged their wrong doing, it will destroy your sense of *self*; self-confidence; self-worth; self-value; self-determination; and self-fulfillment of being everything that you are capable of being.

Forgiveness is not so much meant for the other person. Many times the people that hurt you are so caught up in themselves that they either do not realize they hurt you, do not care that they hurt you, or are too psychologically debilitated to know the difference. Forgiveness allows you the opportunity to release the anchor, find peace in your heart and move forward. I was in an abusive marriage for years and even today I have never understood why I was abused, nor did he ever acknowledge or apologize for it. I used the word "hate" a lot back then. Hate was the only word that truly described how I felt about him and what he had done to me. But I was stuck! In my mind and in my heart I was trapped by the hatred I felt, which made me lose my sense of *self.*

One night on my living room floor I asked God to forgive me for allowing hate to harden my heart, and to forgive my ex-husband for the abuse. It was only a day or two later that I noticed a change, I began to feel much lighter, almost as if a huge weight was lifted off of me. The nagging and aching pains I use to feel that would settle into my heart and stomach disappeared, I dropped my anchor! And because I was willing to forgive, God forgave me for the hatred and lightened heart. Everyone one of us has a story, but regardless of what yours is you have the power and ability to change the ending by releasing forgiveness in your life and moving forward toward bigger and better promises.

"Do not be anxious about anything, by prayer and petition, with thanksgiving; present your requests to God. And the peace of God, which transcends all understanding, will guard your hearts and your minds in Christ Jesus" (Phil. 4.6-7).

Worry and anxiety are key contributors to mental stress in America today. Inge describes worry as "interest paid on trouble before it becomes due" (2). The constant quest for material possessions and then even more constant worry about how to financially maintain what you have, only seeks to add even more stress to the complexities of life. For some happiness is tied to what they own and the overall value of their net worth. For others good health, family, a comfortable home and a deeper connection with God define their level of success. Whatever your quest may be and definition of happiness, the scripture tells us that we are to be anxious for nothing. It is very easy to get caught up in material things allowing possessions to control our sense of value and define our purpose. There are a dozen or more scriptures in the bible that speak to us about worry and anxiousness. The promises of God unequivocally tell us that we are to worry for nothing, because ultimately we have no control over worldly things anyway, but God is in total control of the universe.

Menninger states "The daily pressures to act, to do, to decide, make it difficult to stop and think, to consider, and to examine your life's goals, directions, and priorities to find the best choices you have for managing your own world" (qtd. in Hudson and McLean, 4).

There is nothing wrong with being successful God desires for us to live an abundant life. But often times we allow material possessions to dictate our attitudes and behavior toward others, which devalues the Godliness within. When you allow your accomplishments to distract you from the things of God and more over your ability to maintain a humble perspective about who you are in Christ, then you move away from the will of God. Baxter states "As long as man's main concern in life is material; body, food, clothes, houses, possessions--he is in an uncertain, precarious situation.

There is no other way than the way of anxiety and worry, because the things in which his life is centered are so impermanent and changing. However, the moment that he makes God and his kingdom the spiritual realities central in his life worry and anxiety begin to fade away. When the spiritual becomes dominant in his thinking he finds that he is no longer burdened by the uncertainties of the material things of this life" (1). *"But seek first His kingdom and His righteousness and all these things will be added to you"* (Mt 6.33).

If we truly purpose to move toward a more faith-filled existence then we must examine the basis of our central focus. Worry and anxiety is yet another anchor that holds us back and distracts us from moving forward. When you are stressed about the present circumstances of your life and worried about maintaining your current state of being, then it is virtually impossible to envision the future. In order to free yourself from the burdens of worry you have to first release it to the only one who has total control, and the ability to change your circumstances, God! *"Be anxious for nothing, but in everything by prayer and supplication with thanksgiving let your requests be made known to God"* (Phil 4.6).

- *There is no value in simply planning to do good if you don't actually do it.*

- *Un-forgiveness is like an anchor tied to your ankle that will not allow you to take another step until you release it.*

- *Forgiveness is not meant for the other person!*

- *Worry and anxiety is yet another anchor that holds us back and distracts us from moving forward.*

Your hearts desire

As human beings living in the flesh and desiring carnal things, our thoughts and ideas are often far from that of God. But when you come into relationship with God and purpose to please him he will restructure the desires of your heart to line up with his desires and purpose for your life. This does not mean that what you truly desire will be minimized in any way however, God will place great emphasis on developing the desires of your heart with a greater purpose.

We desire a lot! Let's be real: the world is our toy box full of many things we constantly want, crave and desire, and even that is subject to change at a moment's notice. But what you can't escape is the deepest desire that you suppressed or gave away to defeat, that is still deeply embedded in the depths of your heart. God sees our effort, but more importantly he knows our hearts our minds and our soul. When he searches our hearts to fulfill his promises within us he ensures a successful end. That is not something we typically think of when we desire something, we just know what want. But God's fulfillment of our wants and desires is magnificently planned from beginning to end, with every detail already worked out for our success.

Most people just desire to live a prosperous and satisfied life. God desires the same for us, but with less drama and difficulty. Does that mean you will not experience complications on the road of your successful path, not at all, but it does mean that once you arrive you will enjoy it in a more peaceful and healthy way. The Bible tells us to *"Delight yourself in the Lord and he will give you the desires of your heart"* (Ps. 37.4). Garfield and Eberle suggest six principle concepts to help you embrace your hearts desires:

- *Laughter – God wants us to learn to laugh again. It will heal your heart and renew your love for God and people. Laughter is medicine for our soul.*

A cheerful heart is good medicine, but a crushed spirit dries up the bones (Prov. 17.22).

- *Ask and receive – God connects our joy with learning to receive good gifts from Him.*

  "So I say to you: Ask and it will be given to you; seek and you will find; knock and the door will be opened to you. For everyone who asks receives; he who seeks finds; and to him who knocks, the door will be opened (Luke 11.9-12).

- *Pretend – "Learn to pay attention to your desires, you'll find God there. Begin to pray, Father, I give myself permission to dream about the desires you've placed within my heart. Faith begins with pretending" (Garfield and Eberle).*

  "And whatever things you ask in prayer, believing, you will receive" (Mt. 21.22).

- *Play – "Now, instead of just pretending, begin to confess and act upon your dream. It will feel like play; what you've always wanted to do! If you're going to be the friend of God, you'll have to learn to trust Him to give you the desires of your heart. You have to believe that, "created in His image," means your heart's desires are godly, and that you have authority to speak them into existence, just the way God does" (Garfield and Eberle).*

  "If you abide in me, and my words abide in you, you will ask what you desire, and it shall be done for you" (Jn. 15.7).

- *Have a dream – "Give yourself permission to dream about your heart's desire and then begin to prophesy it into existence: Envision and dream what God has put in our hearts; He pours out his spirit; we Prophesy the dream into existence" (Garfield and Eberle).*

"In the last days,' God says, 'I will pour out my Spirit on all people. Your sons and daughters will prophesy, your young men will see visions, your old men will dream dreams. Even on my servants, both men and women, I will pour out my Spirit in those days, and they will prophesy" (Acts 2.17-18).

- *God has a question for you: (Garfield and Eberle).*

At Gibeon the LORD appeared to Solomon in a dream by night; and God said, "Ask! What shall I give you? (1 Kings 3.5)

Embrace your dreams by creating

goals to get you there

Your success in life begins with the hope and dreams to be whatever you desire to become. When you can envision yourself where you want to be, you have a greater chance of seeing it to fruition. According to Tracy "Goals allow you to control the direction of change in your favor." Having intermediate short and long term goals will make your dreams more realistic and give you a blueprint for your future accomplishments. Our thoughts give us a foundation to proceed toward the achievement of a goal, but when you put it in writing like Habakkuk the promises become revelation and subject to the promises of God as a plan for an appointed time.

The first time I heard my daughter mention college she was about 7 years old. My son was 2 years old and had waited anxiously all day for her to come home from school so they could play together. When the front door opened and she came in he ran up to her, hugged her and said "Danielle let's play." She very sternly looked at him and said "not right now, I have to do my homework first and then we can play." Even then she had a goal in mind for her life. It is inconceivable to me that she knew exactly what her future accomplishments would be, but one thing was very clear; education would be the key to help her achieve her dreams. She was always very self-disciplined and studious, and she maintained honors and perfect attendance consistently.

I remember once she caught the flu and staggered out of bed with a high fever, crying because I did not wake her up for school and she did not want to be late. I said "Danielle you are too sick to go to school today" still crying she said, "but I'm going to miss everything." I couldn't help but laugh to myself, thinking how much coloring and drawing could she actually miss, but her determination was admirable and still is today!

Genesis (37.1-11) tells of how Joseph was loved by his father more than his brothers, which caused jealousy and hatred among them. Joseph was a dreamer and when he told his brothers of his dreams they interpreted it to mean that he would rule over them some day and that they would bow down to him, and the bible say "they hated him all the more." Joseph's bothers conspired to kill him, but ended up selling him into slavery and then telling their father that he was devoured by wild animals. What is amazing about this story is that years later even after all of Josephs' trials and tribulations he was appointed by Pharaoh to have charge over all the land of Egypt, essentially even ruling over his brothers as he dreamed he would.

Our dreams are not misguided irrelevant thoughts, but promises that have been birthed within us early on. Dreams are something to be cultivated and developed through motivation, maturity and growth. When you have birthed a dream for an intended end, nurture and sustain it by establishing a foundation of goals and a plan to help you get there. As life changes so will your plans and sometimes even your dreams, but it does not end there. We have the ability to adapt a new dream and vision at any given time, and if your dreams are interrupted by unexpected changes that have discouraged you from pursuing one dream, then go after another one. A long as your determination is strong and your will to pursue and prosper is resilient, God will make a way for your dreams to take form, eventually even the ones you put aside will resurface in unordinary ways.

Although dreams and goals are sometimes interchangeably used in discussion, they both incorporate different meanings and learning to differentiate the two will help you to manifest them all the more. Webster's defines dreams as "to have an ambition, to conceive of or imagine" (345). Dreams are birthed from imagination, as foresight into our inner most hopes and desires and if conceived or believed as an attainable reality then can be manifested as a self-fulfilling prophesy. Dreams give us a pathway to a desired destination, while goals become the road map of directions, strategies and plans that set us out on that desired path. Scorsone suggest "A great thing happens when you focus your center of attention on your dream destination, you begin to locate and find solutions for the journey along the way, and goals are the means along the way to fully manifesting your dreams" (2).

What people most times fail to realize is that goals are important to our success regardless of how big or small they may be. As dreamers we tend to reach for the stars, go for the gusto. We want big houses, expensive cars, big bank accounts, and elaborate careers. But the reality is if you can't get to work on time now, is it conceivable that you are setting yourself up for success or to be promoted into a better position where you will constantly be late to work. Sometimes cleaning up the small less important issues will help better prepare you for the road to goal achievement glory. The scripture tells us that "when we are faithful with the little things, then God will make us ruler over much more." God will not enlarge your territory or give you more when you have not been diligent in the small things.

"His lord said unto him, well done, good and faithful servant; you have been faithful over a few things, I will make you ruler over many things: enter into the joy of your lord" (Mt. 25.23)

The same is true of your gifts and talents; the scripture says "that your gifts and talents will make room for you." Proverbs says *"A man's gift maketh room for him, and bringeth him before great men"* (Prov. 18.16). It doesn't matter what you do in life, it does not define who you are as much as the diligence and the passion in which you do what you do to please God. Remember he looks at the heart to examine our motives and desires, and when you keep a good attitude about whatever you do then God will promote you right where you are. The development and manifestation of potential requires *firm faith*, not wishful thinking!

- *Your success in life begins with the hope and dreams to be whatever you desire to become.*

Sometimes life's set-backs
are merely a Set-up!

It is inevitable that you will face disappointments along the way in life. There are even times when you finally get through a situation only to have it resurface later, disguised as a new problem. It took me quite some time to realize that God uses adverse situations to teach us valuable lessons that we most times overlook, because we are too focused on just getting through the problem. Another justifiable premise is that sometimes we are just not ready for what's ahead of us, and so God uses our trials to mature and strengthen us and prepare us in spirit, that we may successfully go through situations with clarity of understanding about the lesson it was meant to teach us.

Exodus tells of how the Israelites wandered in the Sinai desert for 40 years. In a time of a desolate environment God found it necessary for the Israelites to be tested and to find for themselves their faith in Him. When they became hungry and thirsty they turned on Moses and blamed him for their woes. When they complained of no meat, God provided quail; when they complained of no bread, manna fell from heaven; when they complained of no water; God tells Moses to strike his staff against a rock and water comes pouring out. After three months the Israelites arrived at the foot of the holy mountain of Sinai. A cloud encompasses the mountain and God descends into the cloud. God calls to Moses and Moses climbs up the mountain. God speaks and delivers to Moses the Ten Commandments. Since Moses is gone for a long time, the people begin to lose faith and want to make a God of their own. In the Bible, Aaron tells them to bring all the gold jewelry they have, and cast it into a mold. Aaron molds it into a golden calf, and the people worship this golden calf.

When Moses returns he is infuriated. He throws down the tablets and they shatter. Then he takes the calf that the people made and he burns it. He grinds the calf to powder and puts it into the people's water and makes them drink it. Once again, he goes up the mountain and writes down the commandments. The Jews continue to wander through the desert toward the Promised Land for the remainder of the 40 years. Moses is allowed to see the Promised Land but not enter. He climbs to the top of Mt. Nebo, which overlooks Canaan. God says to Moses *"This is the land which I swore to Abraham, Isaac and Jacob. I will give it to your offspring. I have let you see it with your own eyes, but you shall not cross there"* (Deut. 34.4).

There are many themes and lessons embedded in The Story of Moses including the greatness of Moses as a visionary, a leader and a prophet. But perhaps the true spirit of this story is to teach us that change and growth can only come when we have learned the skills of patience, adaptation, cooperation and compromise. There is a lesson to be learned in every situation and with every intended interaction. Like the people of Israel we often times spend a better part of our life repeating mistakes and cleaning up messes from lessons we should have learned from previous situations. Think about the last stressful situation you encountered and recall how you reacted while you were going through it. Did you complain, give into the sympathetic "why me" pleas, or did you thank God for bringing you as far as he has. In reflection did you remind yourself that he is in control and honored him with your trust? If you like the Israelites gave in to murmuring and complaining without acknowledging God in your circumstances, chances are you did not get the lesson, prepare to repeat it! God's ultimate plan is to deliver us into the promise land flowing with milk and honey, but he wants to be sure we are ready and mature enough to receive all that he has for us.

"But one thing I do, forgetting what is behind and straining toward what is ahead" (Phil 3.13). Do not allow the past mistakes to keep you wallowing in self-pity and cause you to lose confidence in who you are. You may not be exactly where you want to be in life, but you have the power and ability by faith to even change the direction of your future. God knows every mistake and wrong turn we will take before it actually happens, and he has already planned the perfect comeback. It does not matter how you started out in life, you can have a dynamic finish

and accomplish things you never thought possible. There are many stories in the Bible of people that had rough beginnings in life, or faced tremendous situations, but with every story the end is more spectacular than its beginning, because the Bible further explains God's hand in restoring, uplifting, and altering the destination of those situations to one of promise and prosperity.

The scripture tells us that "God has the final say and authority in all things." Failure is not the final place of purpose in our life, without failures we could not properly gauge our successes. Failure is however an "opportunity" a chance to re-examine the mistakes we have made and re-calculate a new plan of action. Just because you lost momentum temporarily, that does not mean that the dreams and promises that are inside of you are final either, keep hoping. God's word is final and his promises endure forever, after all He has the power to move mountains! When you believe and trust in his power, his strength will empower you to pick yourself up, brush off the self-doubt and disappointment and keep moving toward your destiny. Set-backs are not designed to make you give up, but like the Israelites in the desert God will use difficult situations to test our faith in him.

If you are stagnant or feel like you have been in a desert for entirely too long, chances are somewhere along the way you may have lost sight of your faith, or taken your eyes off God. We tend to get entangled in our problems forgetting all else. Relationship issues, problems in marriage, work related issues, and financial dilemmas are huge situational factors in life and it is easy to see how they can consume us over all other thoughts, sometimes almost to a debilitating end. But when you remain focused on God and his power to change (any) situation and circumstance then he will re-direct your steps toward his promises for you, then unlike Moses you will reach the promise land.

Set-backs are a momentary derailment! We are not meant to live down and defeated! God's plans for your life are far greater than your disappointments, so receive your mistakes, problems and difficulties as an "opportunity" to grow and scrutinize the lessons it was meant to teach you, as merely a set-up for a phenomenal come back! L'Amour states "there will come a time when you believe everything is finished; that will be the beginning" (1). As we grow older we often times we settle into the idea that we have lived the better part of our lives and our mistakes are just part of who we are. But accepting God's forgiveness for our mistakes begins with forgiving our self, and positioning our self for a comeback. If you accept this as reality, then also know that, the second half of your life can be far better than the first half, if you are willing to use the lessons of the past to guide you.

- *There is a lesson to be learned in every situation and with every intended interaction.*

- *God knows every mistake and wrong turn we will take before it actually happens, and he has already planned the perfect comeback.*

- *Set-backs are a momentary derailment!*

Building a Better Relationship with God

Anyone seeking a closer relationship with God first ask the question, how do I connect in reality to the spirituality of God's existence? In other words how does God manifest and become more tangible in my life? Building a better relationship with God and drawing closer to him takes time, patience and most of all faith. The Bible states *"And without faith it is impossible to please God, because anyone who comes to him must believe that he exists and that he rewards those who earnestly seek him"* (Heb. 11.6).

Relationships are not something that are built overnight, after all think about the relationships you have developed this far, most of which took time to cultivate and grow in trust. As you learned to trust and understand the other person your loyalty to them and confidence also grew with time, and became stronger. Faith is something that also has to be developed, and life's circumstances and difficulties will cause you to doubt and constantly question the boundaries of that faith every day. It is usually after all else fails and we have exhausted all our own efforts, and even sometimes taking a hard fall that we realize the other option (God), must be better than what we have experienced so far.

Most parents with teenage children understand this concept, and the challenges that come with getting your teen to see your decisions and advice as tested wisdom. Typically, the normal response is for them to test the alternatives, their way, and it is only when they fail or make bad choices that they are then willing to re-visit the facets of parental advice. As God's children and with much the same tenacity as teens, our decision and choices are made at times with the same strategy, which sometimes fail or fall short of our father's advice. Learning through the word of God is a process of growing and maturing toward the guidance and wisdom of God, and it takes time to fully come to understand and accept it as sound advice. As you begin to develop a better relationship with God through reading the word and connecting it to the realities of life, as difficult situations arise you will notice an increase in your faith, and your trust and loyalty will also manifest. However, if you choose to test the boundaries of wisdom and ignore tested counsel; you will then limit the capacity for your faith to grow and strengthen. Patient endurance and understanding of the word of God are key factors to spiritual growth; when you decide to ignore sound advice (God's instruction); it will be that much harder to draw the connection between reality and the spiritual presence of God in your life.

Many people desiring to understand God and draw closer to him spend endless hours pondering the question "how am I supposed to have a relationship with a being or existence I cannot see?" Whether you have recently come to believe in the concept of a higher being or are someone that has adapted Christianity as a way of life, developing a better relationship with God is yet another phase of your spiritual growth. Understanding God and developing a closer relationship with him begins with reading the word of God "The Bible." The principles and teachings of the Bible are foundational to accepting who he is and what his expectations are for us as believers. Once you have adapted the principles and teachings of the bible as a lifestyle, meaning you begin to incorporate them into your daily routine as a way of living, then the next step is to understand how to talk to God, through prayer.

Most people think prayer is something that has to be this long drawn out theoretical speech, which includes formal verses, and phrases from the bible in order to get God to listen. I have been to many churches and listened to prayers that went on for what seemed like an hour or more because they appeared to be prepared speeches. For a very long time because of hearing how people prayed in church I was afraid to pray. I thought I would sound silly or not say the right things. But God wants us to come to him as humbly as we know how and that usually means from the heart. He does not want us to practice and recite a bunch of passages we do not even understand in hopes that it will make him respond faster to our request. What he does want is your honesty, your effort and your sincerity as you talk (pray) to him.

Prayer is talking to God, earnestly releasing your thoughts, desires, fears and problems to him, in belief that he will give you resolve by faith.

The Bible says "*This, then, is how you should pray: Our Father in heaven, hallowed be your name, your kingdom come, your will be done on earth as it is in heaven. Give us this day our daily bread. Forgive us our debts, as we have also forgiven our debtors. And lead us not into temptation, but deliver us from the evil one*" (Mt. 6.9-13). If prayer is a new notion for you and you are just beginning a relationship with God, use this prayer as a foundation to start talking to Him daily. Once you begin to recite this day-to-day, your heart will begin to open up to other areas of your life that you will want to share with him through prayer and this will deepen your relationship with him over time.

There are many reasons to communicate with God on a daily basis. Whether you see it as an opportunity to release your frustrations or ask for guidance prayer should undoubtedly and always begin with thanksgiving. Thanking and praising God for what he has already done in our lives not only demonstrates our gratitude and trust in him, but also shows that we appreciate and rely on him. Asking for forgiveness and requesting guidance from temptation and evil is another way to demonstrate our devotion to living in the will of God. Then make your request known to him, but keep in mind God is not on our time clock, he works a little different, nor will he answer every request. "*For my thoughts are not your thoughts, neither my ways are your ways declares the Lord*" (Isa. 55.8).

God has carefully planned our successes in his time and in due season, so when you pray it is to unrealistic to expect an immediate result. The scripture tells us "*All a man's ways seem right to him, but the Lord weighs the heart*" (Prov. 21.2). There have been many times in retrospect that I have been glad that God did not answer a specific prayer. At times we are driven by materialism, and wants and desires that do not line up with the will of God, and when we do not receive the answers we are expecting we tend to lose faith, question God and stop praying. But remember his word's "the Lord weighs the heart" and if our heart is not right and in the will of God, then you just may want to considered those unanswered prayers a blessing. God also may not answer every prayer or request in the manner you expect it to come, but know that his comfort and guidance will get you through whatever situation you are facing with the strength to keep moving toward his promises for your life.

Knowing God's will for your life begins with growing in love and developing an attitude that seeks to please him. Adapting a more cooperative and congenial attitude toward others will help you align yourself for Jesus to work through you to extend his love to others, which is pleasing to God. Many of us question whether or not we are doing God's will, but the answer to this question is first answered by understanding the difference between exerting your own will and power over a situation verses following the will of God, which the bible teaches is our guide. When you are truly acting in God's will, you will find peace and experience a sense of safety totally contrary to the frustration and anxiety that comes from doing things your way. The scripture says *"Do not conform any longer to the pattern of this world, but be transformed by the renewing of your mind. Then you will be able to test and approve what God's will is-his good, pleasing and perfect will"* (Rom. 12.2).

Trusting God is the key to spiritual growth. As you begin to develop a better relationship with him through prayer and meditation on the word of God, you will come to understand his will over that of your own. This does not mean you will ignore your own desires or immediately become the perfect Christian doing what is right all the time. We have already established that as humans there is no perfection. But what you will begin to notice is a more peaceful inner spirit and heart, which desires to please God in everything you do. In this you will continuously grow and learn that unanswered or delayed prayers (our will) are truly God's way of orchestrating a better plan (his will) for our good and successful end. Though you may not always understand his plans for your life, if you continue to trust him he will guide you to the promises of your heart's deepest desire.

- *Building a better relationship with God and drawing closer to him takes time, patience and most of all faith.*

- *Prayer is talking to God, earnestly releasing your thoughts, desires, fears and problems to him, in belief that he will give you resolve by faith.*

Learning to Receive God's Correction

Correction is a normal part of growing up in life. From infancy well into adulthood, chances are you have been or will be told that you have done something wrong. Children that receive correction as a healthy part of their development tend to be more obedient and respectful as they mature. Early correction is important because at some point and time a teacher, another parent and boss or significant other will undoubtedly correct you. If you have not learned early in life to receive correction as a normal part of being then receiving it from God may be even more difficult to fathom.

Taking responsibility for our actions is not always an easy thing. Typically it is always easier to believe that the fault is with someone else, but unrealistic in thought. Placing blame and holding someone else responsible for our own actions and behavior discredits us and shows our lack of maturity to learn and grow from our mistakes. Children learn this concept early on, but for different reasons most often blaming someone else for something gone wrong is an escape mechanism, which translates to an escape from punishment. Adults that do not take responsibility are either oblivious to reality or like children are attempting to escape punishment or the consequences of their actions.

The Bible says *"If we confess our sins, he is faithful and just and will forgive us our sins and purify us from all unrighteousness"* (Jn. 1.9). When you fail to take responsibility for your actions you place your self in a precarious situation. How can we be forgiven for things that we are not willing to first admit guilt in, and second seek forgiveness for? When you seek God's forgiveness trust that he has forgiven you, let it go and do not continue to dwell there. Scripture tells us that "God holds nothing from us or against us." God does not hold grudges, but unless you confess your sins and take ownership of your mistakes he cannot forgive what you do not disclose. We tend to become stuck in our minds, which allow us at times to believe that we are no better than the mistakes we have made or the sins we have committed.

The truth is we were derived from sin and are imperfect in nature; some type of act of sin is inevitable. But it does not have to define who you are unless that is where you choose to reside. Remember, we are all subject to free will. God does not force his doctrine on us or coerce us into anything we do not wish to do. But what's amazing about his love for us is that he will never turn his back on you when you finally do decide to seek his forgiveness. Have you ever done something so stupid that even in that moment you knew you were wrong, but thought Ok, I can just fix it later. Sometimes our mistakes can scar us for life and we may find ourselves in situations where we are powerless to go back and make changes, or get a do over. But "God has power and authority over all things" (*say that a few times until it starts to sink in*). When you find your-self at a dead end and have exhausted all of your resources and human capabilities that is usually when we begin to seek God's help. Just know "your promise will have pain" this just means that you will have to suffer through the process of correction to find victory on the other side of it. Before God will move us out of a situation even through correction he must first break us, re-shape us, and build us in character. He does this so we are fully aware that he is at work in our lives, and so that we will not revert back to where or what he has delivered us out of. His presence in your situation will be so profound and recognizable that you will have no choice but to acknowledge and thank him constantly, this is where we begin to come into relationship with him.

When he develops us in character it is a maturing process that takes place within and allows you to reflect back with gratitude instead of regret. God is a phenomenal teacher and when you get the power of instruction from his lessons through your situation then you are ready to be elevated to the next level of glory and promise.

The Bible tells of forgiveness and how we shall forgive our brother who sins against us. *"Peter asked Jesus, Lord how many times shall I forgive my brother when he sins against me? Up to seven times? Jesus's answer was, not seven times, but seventy-seven times; therefore the kingdom of Heaven is like the King who wanted to settle his accounts with his servant"* (Mt. 18.21-23).

"When bought before his master to settle his debt the servant was unable to pay, the servant begged for mercy and the master took pity on him and cancelled the debt. But the servant later ran into another servant that owed him a debt, and the bible says he grabbed him and began choking him and demanded he repay the debt. But the servant refused and had the man thrown into prison, when the other servants heard of this they told the master who had previously forgiven the servant of his debt. The master called the servant in and became angry, he reminded him the mercy he showed him in cancelling his debt, and turned the servant over to the jailers to be tortured until he repaid his debt" (Mt. 18.24-35). This story demonstrates the power of forgiveness, but also how God's correction is at play in teaching the servant a valuable lesson about forgiveness.

There is no monetary fee for God's mercy, his grace or forgiveness. His son Jesus has already paid the price for our prosperity and the forgiveness of sin. Receiving God's correction is how we re-establishing ourselves as being worthy of his righteousness. But just like the servant in Matthew if you do not acknowledge wrong doing and seek forgiveness as an initial step toward forgiveness, correction cannot take place because you have not positioned yourselves to deal with the consequences of that in which correction will bring.

- *Placing blame and holding someone else responsible for our own actions and behavior discredits us and shows our lack of maturity to learn and grow from our mistakes.*

- *When he develops us in character it is a maturing process that takes place within and allows you to reflect back with gratitude instead of regret.*

- *There is no monetary fee for God's mercy, his grace or forgiveness!*

Profound Peace

Inner peace is a journey within itself. The daily grind of work-related stress and family and relationship issues coupled with economics is enough to keep anyone stressed out and uptight. But fortunately for all of us that is not God's plan for our lives. The quest for peace begins with receiving Jesus Christ as our personal savior and surrendering all that you are and are going through over to him. Some may disagree with this concept and may have even given into the mindset that peace is objective in perspective.

One thing is very clear; people define their own peace in different ways. Having all of your bills paid on time will give you a sense of peace. Having a comfortable home life and loving family unit will give you a sense of peace. Getting up in the morning to go to a job you love will give you a sense of peace. But, let's face it the *majority* of people that live in an imperfect world do not have that type of peace and may never experience it without help and guidance.

As a single mother I struggled with worry and stress for a long time, as many do, and I really began to think it was a natural part of life. But it wasn't until I developed a closer relationship with God and learned to turn to him for help, direction and guidance that I began to notice a change in myself. When you fully begin to trust God in all things you will also learn to surrender every worry, every thought, every problem and even all of your hopes and dreams over to his control. Once you can comfortably release your burdens and learn to lean on God, it will feel as if a huge weight has been lifted off of you and a sense of calm will come over you that may make you wonder why nothing seems to bother you anymore.

Surrendering was a concept that baffled me for quite some time and I couldn't help but to expect something to go wrong at any minute, or wonder why the sky hadn't fallen yet. Over time I became more relaxed, less worried or concerned about things I was powerless to change and I trust God to work things out in my favor. When you truly come into a trusting relationship with God, where you are able to cast your cares on him and move forward without a second thought it truly is "peace that surpasses all understanding." The scripture tells us to "*trust in the Lord with all your heart and lean not to your own understanding; in all your ways acknowledge him, and he will make your paths straight*" (Prov. 3.5-6).

Profound peace is an experience, one that settles your spirit and frees your mind to focus on the promises of God, not the daily grind and complications of life. Does that mean you will no longer face problems or strife? Absolutely not! But the manner in which you accept, perceive and handle problems and strife will drastically begin to change you. Webster's defines peace as "inner contentment, serenity and being free from strife" (808). Understanding how to come into a place of peace in your heart, mind and total being will change your life and the way you begin to see the world around you. Most times our discontentment is triggered by strife and chaos caused by dealing with various situations and personalities that are not compatible with your own. Be it a significant other, co-worker, family member or friend it doesn't matter the playing field is all the same. But let's face it God did not create each of us to think alike, act alike or be like anyone else. Our identities and unique personalities are what make us who we are.

People come and go in our life's span, that is the all apart of God's seasonal transition. Not everyone will remain in your existence for the long haul. Nor are you required to befriend people that you are not compatible with. But have you ever heard someone say "you could be entertaining angels?" Also consider that you never know who God may put in your path or for what reason. We are at times too quick to judge and dismiss people that do not fit our mode of thinking and who we typically would not call "friend." I too have been guilty of pre-judging a person's actions or attitude before actually getting to know them. Sometimes, until you get to know another person's story and the reason they are so indifferent, then it may be all the more difficult to accept them for who they are. The effort to accept and understand others allows you to broaden your awareness about them and walk a more peaceful path of love. Now mind you there are two concepts at work here: finding peace in the midst of incompatibility and walking in love.

When you have come into a place of peace and experience total serenity even in the most difficult of times you will be very cautious to guard who you allow into your space as a general rule. When you encounter negativity and strife it will either cause you to give into that behavior because it is so powerful and predominate around you; or you will have the good sense to think, re-examine the effect it has on you and move away from it. Socializing with people that are positive, motivating, uplifting and pleasant will add value to you and impact your behavior and attitude profoundly, if you allow it to. The decision in which perspective you adapt as a lifestyle is up to you, but this choice should be an easy one. No one should want to live in strife and controversy all the times. The world is full of enough difficulties without adding fuel to the fire. Be cautious and selective in who you allow in your space. Ask yourself, is their influence over who you are more powerful than the influence of God, and who he wants you to be? If you are at a point in your life where peace is a foreign place, then you are not in the will of God.

I am typically a very easy going, kind of go with the flow type of girl, to a degree. Don't get me wrong I have never been a follower, and have never been afraid to say no to people or situations that made me uncomfortable. But what's common about going with the flow is that you settle into the complacency of accepting strife or (drama) as part of the norm. The reality is that it does not have to be unless you desire it and allow it into your space. When you have fully grasped this concept then you will come to understand when to just walk away. The Bible says "Great peace-have they who love your law and nothing can make them stumble" (Ps. 119.165).

Often times we allow the actions and motives of others to disturb our peace and stir up feeling of anger and anguish. It took some time before I finally realized that the devil uses people to throw us off track. If he can stir up enough negativity and stress as part of his plan to keep you distracted, he can separate you from the will of God. This is usually not hard to do considering the harshness and insensitivity of the actions of others as the norm. At times peoples moods, attitudes and overall bad behavior have nothing to do with you, it's just that they have not yet discovered "peace." Typically people that are driven by constant difficulties are just looking for a way to release it. Lashing out at others, blaming someone else, and walking in hate and discontent is usually how they choose to do so. Be mindful of the fact that all people are not bad, but bad situations create people that behave badly.

Walking in love is somewhat different from accepting others as a measure of compatibility. Walking in love involves random acts of kindness, a smile or courtesy without reason and not allowing indifferences or the thought of acceptance to create barriers when doing so. Learning this has taught me that I can still show love and kindness to others, even strangers without commitment. I use the word commitment because it always mystifies me that people are afraid to speak and will treat you like an invasive relative if you speak to them, almost as if it were a long term commitment. The suspicion in all of us has caused us to become jaded and on guard against kindness, which creates barriers to walking in love, not just for yourself, but for the person attempting to show you love.

God has amazing plans for each of us. Wouldn't it be nice to wake up each morning knowing you do not have to face your fears or your problems alone? The reality is that you can! Faith opens doors to a new world of peace and promises just waiting for you to receive when you open your heart and mind to the acceptance of Christ Jesus. He is our helper and a shining light through the dark valleys of what we call life. Allow him to move in your life and guide you to a more profound place of peace. *"I will lie down and sleep in peace, for you alone, O Lord, make me dwell in safety"* (Ps. 4.8).

When your spirit is settled the concept of peace will become an expectation through trusting God, which is when you have aligned yourself with his will for a more insightful love walk. It will be difficult to show love and kindness to others without expectation or motive unless you are at peace within yourself first.

I am no theologian by any means, but that is what's so amazing about the word of God. It has the power to impact the lives of ordinary people like you and I every-day through study, synthesis and application. In my quest to understand the Bible better, I read it cover to cover; from Genesis to Revelations and have become passionately inspired to know more and grow more toward the will of God. I cannot say that I fully understood all that I read, after all it is deep in historical facts and words that are hard to pronounce, but as I began to read it my desire to know and understand increased further, as did my desire to be transformed by the renewing of my mind.

Many people go to church regularly, but are waiting on some colossal change within them-selves in order to be good enough to give their lives to God. I used to be one of those people! I would always think, once I fix this or correct that, and then I will go before God. He expects us to come to him as we are. He already knows we are broken, and imperfect. There is nothing that God cannot help you fix within yourself, if you allow him to be your helper.

Your journey can be whatever you desire it to be. Look back over your own life's experiences and examine what it has taught you. After you have taken a quick inventory of where you have been then you can better assess where you are going, and how you will get there. Whatever you choice of direction, I hope that you will open your heart and mind and make God a part of your journey!

- *Profound peace is an experience, one that settles your spirit and frees your mind to focus on the promises of God, not the daily grind and complications of life.*

- *Walking in love involves random acts of kindness, a smile or courtesy without reason and not allowing indifferences or the thought of acceptance to create barriers when doing so.*

-

- *Many people go to church regularly, but are waiting on some colossal change within them-self in order to be good enough to give their lives to God. Accepting salvation begins the process of change.*

References

Adler, R. B. & Elmhorst, J. M. *Communicating at Work: Principles and Practices for Business and the Professions* (11th Ed.). Hightstown, NJ: McGraw-Hill, 2004.

Baker, N. D. Learning Quotations by Newton D. Baker. December 4, 2011. http://quotationsbook.com/quotes/author/404, 2008.

Baxter, B. B. Be Not Anxious For Your Life. Sermon No. 461: Hillsboro Church of Christ. Nashville, Tennessee: Radio Station WLAC, 1965: 1-3.

Blair, G. R. Gary Ryan Blair Quotes. December 4, 2011. http://www.angelfire.com/ma4/memajs/quotes/know.html. 2011. (1).

"Change." Def. 1a.Webster's II New College Dictionary. Boston, MA: Houghton Mifflin Company, 1995.

Covey, S. R. *Seven Habits of Highly Effective People*. Simon and Schuster, 2004.

"Dreams." Def. 2-3.Webster's II New College Dictionary. Boston, MA: Houghton Mifflin Company, 1995.

Eilers, D. Dying to Self. Clarion. December 4, 2011. http://www.clarion-call.org/extras/die/die.htm, 2011.

"Faith." Def. 2.Webster's II New College Dictionary. Boston, MA: Houghton Mifflin Company, 1995.

Garfield, J. & Eberle, H. Learning to be Child-like Six Ways to Find Your Heart's Desire: Releasing Kings for ministry in the Marketplace. December 5, 2011. http://www.releasing-kings.com/hearts-desire.html, 2011.

Herbert-Dune, F. Quotes by Frank Herbert. December 4, 2011. www.goodreads.com/quotes/show/280059, 2008.

Hofner, E. The Passionate State of Mind. December 4, 2011. http://www.quotationspage.com/quote/3207.htm, 1954: 1-3.

Hudson, F. M. & McLean, P. D. Life Launch. "Berrends, Polly, B." Santa Barbara, CA: The Hudson Institute Press, 2006: (28).

Hudson, F. M. & McLean, P. D. Life Launch. "David McNally." Santa Barbara, CA: The Hudson Institute Press, 2006: (xx).

Hudson, F. M. & McLean, P. D. Life Launch. "Dostoyevsky." Santa Barbara, CA: The Hudson Institute Press, 2006: (57).

Hudson, F. M. & McLean, P. D. Life Launch. "Ouspensky, P. D." Santa Barbara, CA: The Hudson Institute Press, 2006: (52).

Hudson, F. M. & McLean, P. D. Life Launch. "Roy Menninger." Santa Barbara, CA: The Hudson Institute Press, 2006: (4).

Illeris, K. Adult education and adult learning. Malabar, FL: Krieger, 2004a.

Inge, William R. BrainyQuote.com. Xplore Inc., 2012. 6 March. 2012: 1-2. http://www.brainyquote.com/quotes/authors/w/william_ralph_inge_2.html

Knowles, M. S. The Modern practice of adult education. From Pedagogy to Andragogy. (2nd Ed.). New York: Cambridge Books, 1980.

L'Amour, L. BrainyQuote.com. Xplore Inc., 2012. 8 March. 2012. http://www.brainyquote.com/quotes/authors/l/louis_lamour.html

"Meditation." Def. 1a-b.Webster's II New College Dictionary. Boston, MA: Houghton Mifflin Company, 1995.

Merriam S, B., Caffarella, R. S. & Baumgartner, L. M. *Learning in Adulthood*. San Francisco, CA: Jossey Bass, 2007.

Mezirow, J. Transformative dimensions of adult learning. San Francisco, CA: Jossey-Bass, 1991.

"Peace." Def. 5. Webster's II New College Dictionary. Boston, MA: Houghton Mifflin Company, 1995.

Pollard, W. William Pollard Quotes. December 4, 2011. http://www.brainyquote.com/quotes/authors/w/william_pollard.html, 1882-1893.

Scorsone, C. Manifesting Dreams: Dreams and Goals-Is There A Difference? December 10, 2011. http://www.dreammanifesto.com/dreams-goals-difference.html, 2009: 1-5.

Spurgeon, C. H. Charles H. Spurgeon Quotes. December 4, 2011. http://www.goodreads.com/author/quotes/2876959.Charles_H_Spurgeon, 2009.

The Holy Bible. New International Version (NIV). Grand Rapids Michigan: Zondervan Publishers, 1973.

Tracy, B. Brian Tracy Quotes Page: Inspiration and Motivation. November 2011. www.personal-development-training.com, 2010.

Triplett, G. Gillis Triplett Ministries: You Were Born to Win. November 2011. www.gillistriplett.com, 2004.

Viniar, B. Quotes Lady's Quotes. December 4, 2011. www.quotelady.com/authors/author-v.html, 2011.

Williamson, M. A Return to Love: Reflection on the principles of a course in miracles. "Our Deepest Fear." Harper Collins. 1992: 190-191.

Wilson, M. Leo Plass Receives Long-Delayed Diploma From EOU. November 2011. www.KTVZ.com, 2011.

Wooden, J. Be Eager to Learn. December 4, 2011. http://www.theteliosgroup.com/quotes/category/lifelong-learning, 2009.

Index

1

1 Corinthians 13
 4-13 60
1 Corinthians 15
 33 53, 54
1 Kings 3.5 80
1 Peter 4
 8 59

2

2 Chronicles 7
 14 46
2 Corinthians 3
 18 65
2 Corinthians 6
 14 53
2 Corinthians 10
 4 40
2 Corinthians 12
 9 63
2 Corinthians 13
 5 46

A

Acts 2.1-4, 17 57
Acts 2.17-18 80

C

Colossians 1
 21 69
Colossians 2
 18 69
Colossians 3
 10 69

D

Deuteronomy 30
 1-10 56
Deuteronomy 34
 4 85

E

Ecclesiastes 3
 1-10 37
 11 36

Ecclesiastes 4
9-12 52
Ecclesiates 3
1 36
Ephesians 2
3 69
Ephesians 3
20 13
Ephesians 4
17 69

G

Genesis (37.1-11) 82

H

Habakkuk 2
2 56
Hebrew 11
6 88
Hebrews 11
1 43
6 22, 44
Hosea 4
6 6

I

II Corinthians 4
4 69
II Corinthians 11
3 69

I Kings 19.12 56
Isaiah 26
3 69
Isaiah 41
10 25
Isaiah 55
8 90

J

James 1.5 64
Jeremiah 1.4-5 3
Jeremiah 17
10 69
Jeremiah 20
12 69
John 1
9 93
John 10
10 21
John 15
7 79
John 16
33 41

L

Luke 11.9-12 79

M

Matthew 6

9-13 90
14-15 74
33 22, 76

Matthew 11

28-29 12

Matthew 16

24-25 67

Matthew 18

21-23 94
24-35 95

Matthew 21

22 79

Matthew 22

37 69

Matthew 25

23 83

P

Philippians 3

13 85
19 69

Philippians 4

6 76

Pillippians 4

6-7 75

Proverbs 3

5-6 63, 97

Proverbs 4

7 19

Proverbs 11

14 53

Proverbs 12

17 23
26 52

Proverbs 13

20 54

Proverbs 14

6 54
8 24

Proverbs 17

22 79

Proverbs 18

16 83
21 23

Proverbs 21

2 90

Proverbs 22

6 18

Proverbs 23

7 40

Psalms 4

8 99

Psalms 37

4 38, 58, 78

Psalms 119

165 98

R

Romans 1

28 69

Romans 8

5, 7 69

Romans 10

10 44

Romans 12

1-2 68

Romans 12;2 91

Ruth 1.16-17 39

T

Titus 1

15 69